P9-CNE-223

	DATE DUE	
	DISCARD	

Native Americans of the Northwest Plateau

Titles in the Indigenous Peoples of North America Series Include:

Native Americans of the Northwest Plateau

Kelly L. Barth

Lucent Books, Inc.
P.O. Box 289011, San Diego, California

Library of Congress Cataloging-in-Publication Data

Barth, Kelly L.
    Native Americans of the Northwest plateau / by Kelly L. Barth.
        p. cm. — (Indigenous peoples of North America)
Includes bibliographical references and index.
    ISBN 1-56006-877-9 (hardback : acid-free paper)
        1. Indians of North America—Northwest, Pacific—Juvenile literature.
[1. Indians of North America—Northwest, Pacific.] I. Title. II. Series.
    E78.N77 B34 2002
    979.5'00497—dc21

2001001467

Printed in the U.S.A.

Contents

Foreword

North America's native peoples are often relegated to history—viewed primarily as remnants of another era—or cast in the stereotypical images long found in popular entertainment and even literature. Efforts to characterize Native Americans typically result in idealized portrayals of spiritualists communing with nature or bigoted descriptions of savages incapable of living in civilized society. Lost in these unfortunate images is the rich variety of customs, beliefs, and values that comprised—and still comprise—many of North America's native populations.

The *Indigenous Peoples of North America* series strives to present a complex, realistic picture of the many and varied Native American cultures. Each book in the series offers historical perspectives as well as a view of contemporary life of individual tribes and tribes that share a common region. The series examines traditional family life, spirituality, interaction with other native and non-native peoples, warfare, and the ways the environment shaped the lives and cultures of North America's indigenous populations. Each book ends with a discussion of life today for the Native Americans of a given region or tribe.

In any discussion of the Native American experience, there are bound to be sim-

ilarities. All tribes share a past filled with unceasing white expansion and resistance that led to more than four hundred years of conflict. One U.S. administration after another pursued this goal and fought Indians who attempted to defend their homelands and ways of life. Although no war was ever formally declared, the U.S. policy of conquest precluded any chance of white and Native American peoples living together peacefully. Between 1780 and 1890, Americans killed hundreds of thousands of Indians and wiped out whole tribes.

The Indians lost the fight for their land and ways of life, though not for lack of bravery, skill, or a sense of purpose. They simply could not contend with the overwhelming numbers of whites arriving from Europe or the superior weapons they brought with them. Lack of unity also contributed to the defeat of the Native Americans. For most, tribal identity was more important than racial identity. This loyalty left the Indians at a distinct disadvantage. Whites had a strong racial identity and they fought alongside each other even when there was disagreement, because they shared a racial destiny.

Although all Native Americans share this tragic history they have many distinct differences. For example, some tribes and individuals sought to cooperate almost immediately with the U.S. government while others steadfastly resisted the white presence. Life before the arrival of white settlers also varied. The nomads of the Plains developed altogether different lifestyles and customs from the fishermen of the Northwest coast.

Contemporary life is no different in this regard. Many Native Americans—forced onto reservations by the American government—struggle with poverty, poor health, and inferior schooling. But others have regained a sense of pride in themselves and their heritage, enabling them to search out new routes to self-sufficiency and prosperity.

The *Indigenous Peoples of North America* series attempts to capture the differences as well as similarities that make up the experiences of North America's native populations—both past and present. Fully documented primary and secondary source quotations enliven the text. Sidebars highlight events, personalities, and traditions. Bibliographies provide readers with ideas for further research. In all, each book in this dynamic series provides students with a wealth of information as well as launching points for further research.

Hunters and Gatherers of the Northwest

The Plateau region of North America is a two-hundred-thousand-square-mile area of deep forest, valleys, canyons, and meadows to the north and plains and desert with sagebrush and rock to the south. Its boundaries stretch from central British Columbia in Canada south through the United States to eastern Oregon and Washington and most of northern Idaho and northwest Montana.

Though still less developed and populated in comparison to the rest of the United States and British Columbia, the area has significantly changed in the last century. Vast expanses of grassland have been plowed into fields for growing crops such as wheat and potatoes. The region's forests are logged for timber. Lands where animals such as deer once predominated are fenced and managed as rangeland for herds of cattle and sheep. And the region has spawned modern cities with names such as Spokane (Washington), Coeur d'Alene (Idaho), and Lillooet, British Columbia, derived from the names of the indigenous people who first settled there thousands of years ago.

Many members of the Plateau tribes that once thrived in the region live there today, some on reservations and some in the cities that sprang up over the last two centuries. Many tribes such as the Salish (Flathead), Spokane, Yakima, Nez Percé, Coeur d'Alene, Umatilla, Cayuse, Walla Walla, Thompson, and Lillooet are still well represented in the area, but some smaller tribes no longer exist or were combined with larger ones.

Origins of the Plateau Lifestyle

Centuries before the arrival of European settlers to the Plateau region, these native people lived interesting and sometimes difficult lives, governed primarily by the cyclical blooming of plants and fruits and the seasonal arrival of salmon and other fish that thrived in the rivers and streams flowing through the region. Though primarily hunters and gatherers, many people in the tribes also served as healers, artisans, and tribal and religious leaders.

Archaeological evidence suggests that thousands of years ago, the native people began holding trade fairs at central locations. With the arrival of the horse in the region in the 1600s, Plateau tribes expanded their trade to include items acquired from distant Plains tribes and from Europeans as well. Over time, these annual exchanges of food and goods became quite sophisticated, as the various tribes developed specialties not available elsewhere.

Changes in the Plateau Lifestyle

In the eighteenth century, the Plateau region attracted more white hunters, trappers, and explorers, including Meriwether Lewis and William Clark on their famous expedition. The Plateau Indians were interested not only in the goods these strangers could trade but also in their written language and religion. This interest brought a huge number of both Catholic and Protestant missionaries from the East to the region. Some missionaries tried to persuade the Plateau tribes to shift from a hunting and gathering culture to one of raising animals and growing crops. Many also tried to change the Native Americans' dress, habits, religious beliefs, and way of life and convert them to Christianity. With

this mingling of outside cultures came the seeds of future conflict.

Like most Native Americans, the Plateau tribes deeply believed that they had a physical connection with the land. Too-hool-hool-zote, a Nez Percé leader, describes the Native Americans' understanding of their relationship to the land: "The earth is part of my body . . . I belong to the land out of which I came. The earth is my mother."[1] Thus, although the various tribes moved

These Nez Percé chiefs lived in an area of Washington state that is still populated by the tribe today.

Plateau Indians, like this Cayuse tribesman, believed they had a physical connection to the land but did not believe they possessed it.

them goods to trade, crops to grow, and animals to raise. They also brought smallpox, measles, and other contagious diseases against which the Indians had no immunity. Whole villages were wiped out by epidemics of such diseases. As their populations diminished, Plateau tribes found themselves again and again in conflicts over land.

Struggle to Adapt

After a series of ultimately unsuccessful battles to defend their traditional homelands in the Plateau region, one by one, each tribe was beaten by U.S. government and volunteer forces and moved onto reservations. Plateau tribes had to struggle to adapt to a life of confinement to a small land area, since their lifestyle was built around constant travel to follow the seasonal migrations of animals and the ripening of plants over a large area. Some Native Americans had limited success on the early reservations, but even now many are unemployed and depend on government subsidies for survival.

about in certain traditional territories, they did not think that they possessed the land on which they lived. This conviction put the Indians at odds with white settlers, who believed that land could be owned; moreover, many whites believed that they could rightfully take by force any land already occupied by native people.

Drawn by news of large tracts of "unsettled" land in the Northwest, waves of settlers moved into the area, bringing with

Conflicts over rights to water and land, which have plagued the Plateau region for centuries, continue to arise, taking new and ominous forms: Vast areas in and around reservations have been used as disposal areas for hazardous wastes, and rivers have been dammed to create reservoirs for nearby cities. Plateau tribes have fought many legal battles over rights to fish and gather plants in the traditional hunting and gathering areas that remain.

Maintaining Tradition

Despite their struggles, Plateau tribes have tried to maintain links to their religious and cultural traditions and continue to grow in number and political influence. They have developed industries such as forestry, agriculture, and livestock breed-

ing and management to keep the tribes economically healthy. As Julia Davis, a member of the Nez Percé tribe says, they have not forgotten their past and continue to fight battles as their ancestors did to maintain tribal sovereignty and identity: "We as a people are still fighting. We're fighting for our heritage. We're fighting to keep ourselves strong and we have so many battles ahead of us. And our children need to be proud of who they are and what they stand for."[2]

Chapter 1

Pursuing Seasonal Bounty

Until roughly 1850, the Northwest Plateau region was rich in fish, animals, trees, and edible plants that provided year-round food, shelter, and clothing for the people who lived there. To the north, the Plateau region is characterized by evergreen-forested mountains broken by valleys, canyons, and meadows. In this portion, which encompasses present-day central British Columbia, northern Idaho, and eastern Washington, lived the tribes who spoke tribal dialects of the Salish language. These tribes, sometimes called Salishan, included the Kootenai, Coeur d'Alene, Spokane, Colville, Flathead, and others.

Salishan Tribes

The five main Salishan tribes of present-day British Columbia, collectively referred to as the Interior Salish, were the Thompson, Nicola, Lillooet, Shuswap, and Okanagan. These peoples occupied rugged terrain east of the Coast Mountain range in villages scattered along the Thompson, Fraser, and Nicola Rivers.

Among the tribes in the northern portion of the Plateau, the Flathead was one of the largest and most peaceful. They lived primarily in the foothills of the Bitterroot Mountains of western Montana. White settlers used the name "Flathead," a crude reference to the people's natural-shaped heads. The term distinguished these inland people from coastal Salish-speaking tribes to the west, who tied padded boards to their children's foreheads, a practice that resulted in adults with tapered, almost pointed heads. The Flatheads made a striking visual impression of their own to visitors in the area. The website of the Indian Tribal Congress says that the men of the tribe combed their hair so that it "turned up from the forehead, similar to that of the Crows."[3] Although "Flathead" is used in historical contexts, the people today call themselves the Salish tribe.

A close neighbor and associate of the Flathead, the Kootenai tribe, occupied territory that spanned the borders of the present-day United States and British Columbia. In Canada, the name is spelled "Kootenay." For generations, the Kootenai were primarily fishermen, but when they acquired horses from neighboring Plains tribes, their lifestyle changed to one resembling those Plains tribes who pursued herds of buffalo and built tepees.

To the east of the Flathead and Kootenai tribes, the Spokane tribe occupied about 3 million acres of wooded and grassy hills along the Spokane River through eastern Washington, northern Idaho, and western Montana. Originally, the tribe consisted of three bands called the upper, middle, and lower bands— names that corresponded to their position along the Spokane River. *Spokane* means "sun people" or "children of the sun."

Another tribe that depended heavily on the Spokane River was the Coeur d'Alene. They were a peaceful tribe with semipermanent settlements at the headwaters of the Spokane River in northern Idaho near the present-day city of Coeur d'Alene.

Sahaptin Tribes

To its south, the Plateau region changes to an area of hills, plains, and rock formations. Tribes in this region spoke individual tribal dialects of a language called Sahaptin and included the Yakima, Umatilla, Walla Walla, Cayuse, Palouse, Nez Percé, and others. This area covered present-day southeastern Washington, southern Idaho, and eastern Oregon.

The most famous of the Sahaptin tribes called themselves Nimipu, or "the people." French trappers traveling in their territory in Idaho and Washington, however, called them Nez Percé. This French phrase for "pierced nose" fit at the time, since the people wore bone and shell ornaments in their noses. The style, adopted from coastal tribes at

Tribes of the Plateau

Spokane Landscape

Author David Wynecoop noted in his work, "Children of the Sun: A History of the Spokane Indians" that many European visitors to the Spokane territory were awed by its beauty. In his diaries, Belgian-born Catholic missionary Father Peter DeSmet described the region occupied by the Spokane tribe before it was settled and altered by the farms, herds, and cities of settlers. Though no photographs exist of the region before European settlement, DeSmet's description paints a vivid picture of the area.

"The distance from Fort Walla Walla to the great Spokan Prarrie, through which the Spokan river flows, is about 150 miles. This whole region is undulating and hilly, and though generally of a light soil, it is covered with a rich and nutritious grass, forming grazing fields where thousands of cattle might easily be raised. It is almost destitute of timber until you are within thirty miles of the Spokan Prarrie, where you find open woods and clusters of trees scattered far and wide; this portion, particularly, contains a great number of lakes and ponds with ranges of long walls of large basaltic columns and beds of basalt. The country abounds in nutritious roots (bitter-root, camas, etc.,) on which principally the Indians subsist for a great portion of the year. The Spokan Prarrie is about thirty miles from north to south and from east to west, bounded all around by well-wooded hills and mountains of easy access."

trade fairs, was temporary, but the name stuck. In the 1700s, the Nez Percé trapped horses migrating into their territory from the south, where they had been brought to North America by the Spanish. The Nez Percé earned a reputation for being fine horse trainers and breeders, and developed the breed now called Appaloosa.

The Yakima tribe, of central Washington, lived in a series of foothills and ridges along the eastern slopes of the Cascade Mountains, with sacred Mount Adams, or "Pahto," as the Yakima called it, rising from the center of their territory. Yakima legend says that a beaver, or "Wîshpush," created the bed of the Columbia River, which contained ancient floodwaters that flowed through Yakima territory and down to the Pacific.

Three tribes—the Umatilla, Walla Walla, and Cayuse—were so closely associated that they are often discussed as a group. Though each tribe occupied their favorite camping spots, they all hunted deer and other mammals in the same area east of the Columbia River in the Blue Mountains of northeast Oregon and southeast Washington. The Umatilla and Walla

Walla tribes' permanent winter settlements were in the more open, dry areas of sagebrush and juniper toward the lower regions of the Columbia River and its willow- and grass-lined tributaries. The Umatilla frequented the Umatilla River, and the Walla Walla depended more upon the Snake River. The Cayuse occupied a territory farther upstream on the upper courses of rivers such as the Tucannon and Touchet, which drained into the Columbia.

The Plenty of the Rivers

All of the life in the region, especially that of the Native Americans, thrived because of the rich network of rivers crossing the Plateau terrain. The Columbia Plateau, the largest geographic feature of the region, is divided by the Columbia River, which, along with the Fraser River to the north, gives rise to many smaller rivers or tributaries. Many of these rivers, such as the Snake, Clearwater, Boulder, Salmon, Beaverhead, and Cascade, were named for what they looked like or for what could be found within them.

Though the Plateau tribes both hunted game and gathered edible plants and roots throughout the area, they relied principally on fishing during seasonal migrations of salmon, called runs, up the Columbia, Fraser, and Snake Rivers and their tributaries. For many of the tribes, fish made up more than three-fourths of their diet. Along with the primary migratory stocks of salmon also swam steelhead and other types of trout, sturgeon, sucker fish, whitefish, and lamprey eels, which thrived in the clear, cold, and oxygen-rich waters of the Plateau. These rivers provided much more habitat and food than the slow-moving, murky waters of the Plains region, where tribes depended much more heavily on large game.

The salmon was the first food to appear in the Plateau region in early spring. The salmon moved through the rivers again in June and then again in the fall. From each tribe, family bands gathered along the rivers at favorite ancestral fishing sites, such as the Wenatshapam for the Nez Percé, to catch enough salmon to use for the year ahead. During the runs, the fish traveled up every creek and river that emptied into the Columbia.

Catching the Salmon

The tribes used several methods for catching the salmon besides the more familiar method of using poles, hooks, and line. One of the most common and easiest methods of catching salmon was spearing them. The Nez Percé created spears with eight-foot shafts to which they attached three soft prongs, or gigs, of flexible wood such as hackberry. They then pushed carved bone pins into the ends of the prongs. A spear was not thrown in but "jabbed down into the water, the spread of the three prongs adding to its efficiency."[4] The prongs pierced and cradled the bodies of the fish until the men could pull them out of the river. The men of the tribes would hunt by the light of pitch torches; the light attracted the salmon to the area. The men would stand atop towers or rocks

The Plateau tribes' main food source was salmon, which they fished from nearby rivers.

over an area where they had constructed weirs, or mesh, of pliable willow branches, which slowed the fish down long enough to spear them.

Netting was another favored method of catching salmon. For example, the Umatilla constructed long-handled nets woven and attached to flexible wooden hoops. Called dipnets, these tools are still used today by tribal members to catch salmon. The Plateau tribal men often constructed platforms of wood and suspended them from rocks or bluffs near the river's edge. Fishermen stood on these platforms

and leaned over the water, scooping up salmon with their dipnets. Sometimes the men would stand on these platforms and shoot at the salmon with bows and arrows with cords attached.

Though much of the salmon was eaten fresh, much of it also had to be prepared and stored to provide a supply of food throughout the long, cold winters. First, the women butchered the salmon and hung the carcasses on scaffolding or on long racks to dry in the sun or smoked them over fires. Once prepared, the salmon would be stored in containers made from

A Dangerous Way to Fish

The Lillooet, Thompson, and Shuswap tribes of present-day British Columbia often built platforms out over the water, from which they could dip their nets in and scoop up salmon. Fishing in this way, native men caught hundreds of fish per hour at fishing sites that passed from father to son for generations. The netting method was not without its dangers, as anthropologist Brian Hayden illustrates in the book *A Complex Culture of the British Columbia Plateau*:

"Fishing in this fashion was frequently dangerous, especially when several large salmon weighing up to 30 or 40 kilograms each struck the large traditional hoop nets. Fishermen took their lives into their hands when they stood on narrow ledges or springy platforms to catch salmon. Having a rope tied around the waist and secured to something on land saved

many fisherman from plunging into the roiling currents of the Fraser River, a river that sucked people under the water and sometimes did not return them to the surface for days, many kilometers downstream. . . ."

Some plateau tribes employed a dangerous method of fishing that involved netting the fish while leaning over the water.

bark, woven grasses, or other natural materials.

Camas Digging

Equally important as the annual salmon runs for most tribes was the seasonal ripening and blooming of edible roots and plants that grew in the meadows, especially the camas plant, which has blue flowers blooming on erect stalks that can reach three feet in height. Chief Joseph Seltice of the Coeur d'Alene described the sight of the fields: "When the camas was flowering, the entire valley of Potlatch turned a bluish color and was a beautiful sight in the early days."[5] The bulbs are round and the size and shape of medium to large onions, but when eaten raw, they taste a bit like turnips. Plateau tribes ate much of the camas fresh and then prepared the rest for winter storage, for a good camas harvest meant that the people would have enough to eat for the winter.

For about six weeks of the summer while the men and boys hunted for elk and deer, the women used diggers with long wooden handles and carved elk horn shovels to dig the camas roots out of the ground. The children collected and cleaned the bulbs. Then, in a camas steaming pit used each year, the women and children would build a fire to heat a bottom layer of stones. Atop the hot stones, they placed alternating layers of camas bulbs and then grass and moss. When the pit reached ground level, the women poured water over it to steam the bulbs. Once steamed, the bulbs become juicy and sweet. Many were then dried and pounded using a stone mortar and pestle and then shaped into flat cakes for easier storage.

An Abundance of Edible Plants

In summer, the roots of the then-plentiful kouse plant were also dug from the hillsides of the Plateau region. These roots, which tasted like turnips when small and like celery when larger and more ripe, were pounded into biscuits—which gave rise to the plant's common name of biscuitroot—and laid out on woven grass mats to dry.

In the fall, an abundance of wild fruits and plants were ready for harvesting. Women picked huckleberries that could be eaten fresh, boiled into a puddinglike dish, or dried for later use. Chokecherries were pounded with dried deer or elk meat or salmon to make a winter staple called pemmican. Plateau tribal women also harvested serviceberries, bitterroot, wild carrot, sunflower seeds and the sunflower's sweet inner stem, rose hips, currants, and wild onions. In the northern half of the region, even a black moss could be collected from pine and fir trees for baking into a cheeselike substance.

Though the Plateau people rarely went hungry, supplies of such food waxed and waned. Each thing that they ate had to be found in different places, and each was available only in certain seasons. This meant that the Plateau tribes had to move from place to place from season to season, following the supply of food. Also, they had to prepare it where they found it, either to be eaten fresh or to be saved and packaged into containers for winter storage. Year after year, Plateau tribes followed the same course in a large circle, from the lowlands along the rivers to the highlands in the foothills and mountains. Nothing went to waste. The bones and horns of animals were made into tools such as spear tips, digging tools, or spoons. Hides were fashioned into clothing.

Clothing of the Tribes

Though some cloth was made from shredded plant fibers such as sagebrush, cedar, and willow, most of the Plateau tribe wore clothing made from the pelts of the elk and deer they killed during hunting expeditions. They skinned and tanned the pelts of these animals to prepare them for wearing. However, for some winter moccasins, they left the fur as a lining. For the most part, men's clothing consisted of a long buckskin shirt, leggings, belt, a breechcloth or a type of apron, moccasins, and a robe. Women generally wore long buckskin dresses, leggings reaching to the knees, moccasins, and belts. Decoration of clothing was done by dyeing with natural pigments made from things such as roots and berries and attaching porcupine quills and beads.

A Flathead Buffalo Hunt

In the 1880s, while employed by the federal government as Indian agent to the Flathead tribe, Peter Ronan witnessed a buffalo hunt. It was a rare occurrence that the tribe could corner a herd of buffalo in hostile Blackfoot territory. Naturally, doing so was considered quite an accomplishment and caused great excitement in the tribe. The Flatheads would first send scouts out to find and stampede the buffalo back to a corral they constructed to hold them. According to Ronan, who described the event in his book *Biographical Sketch of the Flathead Indian Nation*, the Wah-Kon, an old man believed to have supernatural powers, "plants the medicine mast in the center of the park, and attached to it the three charms which are to allure the animals in that direction . . . a streamer of scarlet cloth two or three yards long, a piece of tobacco and a buffalo's horn." The scouts then took the Wah-Kon's ball, made of hair and covered in skin, from him. The Wah-Kon fasted until the ball was returned to him. As the buffalo were herded into the vicinity of the corral, one scout covered himself in a buffalo hide and imitated the bawling of a calf to lure the herd into the corral. Once the herd was contained in the corral, the rest of the tribe killed them with lances and shot them with bullets and arrows.

Depending on the tribe, clothing varied somewhat. For example, in the winter, men from the Spokane tribe wore a fur hat. For ceremonies, they wore a short, feathered bonnet. Also, Nez Percé women wore conical hats woven from grasses found in the area, and they and the Coeur d'Alene women wore fringed deerskin dresses, decorated with beads or porcupine quills. Their heavily beaded leggings opened at the side and fastened with strings.

Plateau Dwellings

As it supplied the tribes with plentiful food and clothing, the Plateau area also provided ample natural building materials for their dwellings. The earth lodge, or pit house, was a very basic form of shelter dug out of the ground. Poles were laid across the hole and then mats of woven grasses laid across the poles for a roof. A hole was left for smoke to escape and a ladder positioned near it for entering and exiting. Used by the Interior Salish tribes, these lodges were dug out of sandy earth in a circle about thirteen feet wide, which, though small, were very practical because they provided winter shelter. They were used primarily as a place to keep warm and rest during the long winter without burning off excess calories. In fact, the tribes spent most of the winter months in the pit house snuggling and resting, almost as if hibernating.

The Interior Salish pit houses were not only small but also very crowded, with generally only two to three meters of floor space for each person. As many as twenty people might live in such a dwelling. Anthropologist Brian Hayden says that "such a dense press of people is unthinkable for today's industrial citizen. For personal interest, try to estimate the amount of floor space per person you have in your home. Then measure the room you are in to determine how many people would live in it if it were a pit house."[6] However, the close proximity of many bodies served a practical purpose: It provided a daily source of heat. Because of the risk of smoke inhalation, only on the coldest winter nights did natives build a fire in a pit house.

Conical lodges, used by many Plateau tribes, were similar to the earth lodges in that they were built partly underground for increased warmth. Seven to nine poles were stacked around a central pole, then covered with mats woven of cattail. In shape, the structures resembled Plains tepees. In the winter, the conical lodge could be covered with additional cattail mats and built partially underground with dirt packed around the outside to prevent the entry of cold air and wind. Some were as large as thirty feet across.

Larger than the conical lodge, the communal longhouse allowed a group made up of related families, called a band, to live together under one roof. Shaped like a long, narrow version of modern A-frame buildings, these lodges were wooden frames made up of a central ridgepole running the top length of the building, support poles that leaned against and were lashed to the ridgepole, and mats woven of cattail and highly

Many Plateau tribes dwelled in conical lodges that were built partially underground and covered with mats.

rain-repellent tule tied down to the support poles. Tule is described as "skinny-leafed . . . plants [that] grow along rivers and ponds. They were gathered, dried and strung together to make mats."[7] To waterproof the inside of the longhouse, bands lined the interior with animal skins. In a diary of the Lewis and Clark expedition, Meriwether Lewis reported seeing two Nez Percé longhouses that housed thirty-eight families. One was 156 feet long and 15 feet wide. Lewis further explained its construction:

Ultimately, the tepee became the shelter preferred by the Plateau Indians because it was portable.

"The vast interior is without partitions, but the fire of each family is kindled in a row along the middle of the building about ten feet apart."[8] The roof poles did not meet exactly at the top, but instead rested on the horizontal support poles, leaving about one foot of space along the top length of the lodge to allow smoke to escape.

Portable Housing

To increase seasonal mobility, many tribes, such as the Spokane, Nez Percé and Okanagan, began using a lighter, more temporary version of the long-house for hunting and gathering trips. When a band was ready to move on to another camp, the tule mats could be easily rolled up and taken with them. They usually left the longhouse's poles behind because it was much easier to have a readied set of poles at each camp than to carry the heavy frame with them. A large section at the rear of the lodge was often set aside especially for drying salmon on racks.

In the 1700s, with the increase in horse riding and more frequent hunting trips into the Plains, many Plateau tribes began to construct the more familiar tepee. However, early Plateau tribe tepees typically were still covered with tule mats, for the tribes did not have a plentiful supply of large buffalo skins to cover them with, as the neighboring Plains tribes did. As eastern Plateau tribes such as the Nez Percé became more mobile and made more hunting trips into the Plains territory, however, they began to trade for more buffalo hides to cover their dwellings. The tepee became the preferred dwelling because it was so portable and easy to take down. During the 1800s, most of the tribes took tepees along with them when they traveled to the seasonal fairs where all the Plateau tribes gathered to trade wares, race horses, play games, and court each other.

Chapter 2

Tribal Interactions

Plateau peoples had highly complex and organized societies. Their lives as hunters and gatherers required great cooperation both within and between tribes if all were to survive the difficult Northwestern winter. Citing evidence of this cooperation, archaeologists and historians say that for centuries, Plateau tribes gathered at one of several locations in the late summer and early autumn for seasonal food gatherings and trade fairs.

Seasonal Trade Fairs

One of the most famous of the trade fairs took place each autumn along the lower Columbia River where it carves a gorge through the Cascade Mountain range, at the site of the present-day city of The Dalles, Oregon. At this rendezvous site, positioned roughly between the Coastal and Plateau areas, the cultures of the Pacific Coast and the Plains as well as the Plateau could trade and buy things they could not obtain themselves. For example, the Plateau tribes traded their unique wares for ornamental shells from the Northwest Coast tribes and buffalo hides and dried meat from the Plains tribes. The currency used was called "Haiqua," a Chinook word for dentalium—a shell harvested by Coastal tribes off the shores of Vancouver Island and the material from which the currency was made.

Tribes whose permanent winter settlements were near The Dalles—the Wasco and the Wishram—acted as mediators between the various cultures at trade fair time. They could do so because they spoke not only their own language but also those dialects spoken by each of the tribes.

The Dalles site was a highly traveled area during seasonal migrations of the tribes as they moved from fishing to hunting and plant-gathering sites. Because of this, it provided a central gathering point within a range of such communal hunting and gathering sites on or near the Columbia River and the plains of the Columbia Basin. For thousands of years, the same bands, or smaller family groups within the larger tribes, repeatedly used these sites. Though various tribes such as the Cayuse and the Umatilla lived within the area, they "crossed paths, associated freely and traversed and shared each others' subsistence territories at will. All friendly bands were permitted the privilege of use of the others' lands."[9]

It is no coincidence that trade fairs, such as the one at The Dalles, took place in autumn at the end of the typically bountiful summer salmon runs. For many Plateau tribes, salmon was a valuable trading and bargaining tool, since most other tribes—except those in the Plateau area—did not have access to this rich, nutritious meat.

Though The Dalles was the largest, two other sites served as gathering sites for trade fairs. Celilo Falls, also on the lower Columbia River, near the junction of the

Specialized Trade Wares

Each tribe specialized in crafting several particular items to trade at The Dalles. For example, the Nez Percé were well-known for their bags woven of natural fiber, such as hemp and bear grass, into beautiful geometric patterns. They also made long, flat bags out of corn husks, acquired from the Plains tribes, which could be worn over the shoulder and used to collect camas bulbs and other seasonal plants.

Women of the Wasco tribe were also famous for their bags. One cylindrical bag made from soft hemp for root collecting was called a Wasco bag or a "Sally bag."

The Klikikat tribe of present-day British Columbia was famous for their baskets made from cedar roots and designed to collect roots, berries, or other fruit. Coiled very tightly, some of these baskets could be wedged into the ground and used to boil water when fire-heated stones were dropped into them.

Coastal tribes brought seal meat, sturgeon, shellfish, whale blubber, and shells—all items in high demand from the landlocked Plateau tribes.

Plains tribes traded many items highly valued by the Plateau tribes. For example, though the Plateau people could make headdresses, the Sioux made better ones. Soft and heavily beaded and quilled buffalo robes made by the Crow brought a large price.

In turn, Plains Indians traveled many miles to buy or trade for items available only to Plateau tribes. These included salmon oil, pemmican, camas and berry cakes, hemp, beads, pipes, eagle tail feathers, and sheep horns. Highly desired was the Nez Percé bow, made of sheep horn and sinew, which Plains Indians believed was far superior to theirs in accuracy and ease of use.

Deschutes River, was another trading center frequented as late as 1957, when it was flooded by construction of a dam. Before the 1700s and the introduction of the horse, travelers reached both Celilo Falls and Kettle Falls, another trade fair site, by portaging their canoes over river rapids.

Recreation and Socializing at the Fair

These seasonal gatherings provided an opportunity not only to secure food and supplies for the coming winter, but also to have fun and socialize. Competition, especially among young boys, was particularly keen, since prowess in games allowed them to demonstrate power and skill and improve their status in the tribe. Indians collected materials they found around them to use in their games. For example, in one common game, Plateau children tried to throw pinecones through rolling hoops made from grasses, reeds, or bent branches. Indians played a ball game similar to hockey, with curved sticks and buckskin balls stuffed with buffalo hair.

Much socializing went on at trade fairs as well, with relationships begun at these events often leading to marriage. In fact, intermarriage among Plateau tribes was commonplace and had wide-ranging effects both before and after the coming of the white people. According to the Umatilla website, the ease with which tribes intermarried "probably accounted for the fact that no one tribe held claim and boundary to large geographic regions, except for that of traditional occupation and accustomed

and frequent use, such as a winter camp site or spring fishing site."[10] Perhaps for this reason as well, the Plateau tribes, for the most part, defined the roles of men and women in very similar ways.

Roles of Women and Men

With the exception of the Yakima, in which both the husband's and wife's parents were considered blood relatives, lineage in all the other Plateau tribes always derived from the husband's side of the family. However, this did not diminish the respect accorded to women within their band. For example, the food gathered and the utensils created by Yakima women gave them power and prestige and could be given as gifts to honor another woman in the band, who would gain power for herself in the process. Also, Nez Percé women could speak out at tribal meetings, disagree with their father or husband, and even choose their own mate. In general, Plateau women served useful roles, performed demanding tasks, and were treated well accordingly.

Women in the Plateau tribes not only fulfilled their roles as wives and mothers, but also did many of the most demanding tasks. They made all the mats, bags, baskets, and other containers; cleaned and tanned the hides; sewed clothing and made mats or skins used to construct the dwellings; gathered fuel for the fires; dug roots and gathered plants and fruits; and prepared the meals. In the British Columbia tribes of the Shuswap, Thompson, and Lillooet, men often took as many as ten

Plateau women had many responsibilities, including making containers, cleaning and tanning hides, making clothing, and collecting plants and roots.

wives to help with the huge task of butchering and drying the salmon caught during seasonal runs. One Plateau woman could prepare as many as fifty to sixty salmon each day.

Men, on the other hand, generally performed tasks that required traveling away from their families: hunting, fishing, and making war when necessary. Though men spent much of the winter with the rest of the tribe, the tasks they performed around home, such as making arrows, weapons, and tools for the hunt and looking after the horses, usually prepared them for travel.

Plateau Child Rearing

Until Plateau babies were weaned, they were almost continually with their mothers. To keep their hands free to continue working, mothers carried their babies on their backs in wooden cradle boards, called by the Nez Percé "im pol aih," or in baby bags made of deer skin. These cradle boards were padded with skins or plants to cushion the baby's body from bruising. The Yakima used a "Skingah," or hoop of rosebush or other flexible shrub, and fixed it around the baby's forehead to keep the head from rocking side to side as the mother went about her daily tasks. Babies often remained with the mother, daily strapped to the cradle board until they were weaned, usually at age three.

Once a mother had weaned a child, she no longer had sole responsibility for the care of the child; child rearing was a communal task assigned to all tribe members. Misbehaved children were scorned by the whole tribe, so children learned quickly to obey their elders. This does not mean that the Plateau tribes treated their children badly. Indeed, Pend d'Oreille elder Mary Ermitinger says that the tribal members "loved their children without restraint and pampered them as much as was practical."[11]

Plateau babies were carried on their mothers' backs in wooden cradle boards until they were weaned.

As children grew, they were encouraged to excel at the tasks reserved for their gender. To reinforce excellence, a tribe's best hunter would eat a boy's first kill or fish catch, and the highest-ranking woman in the tribe would eat the first roots and berries a girl collected. In the Yakima tribe, when a boy did a man's job, he was thereafter called "winsh." A girl was called "tmay" after her first menstrual period. By their late teens, many boys could fight in wars alongside the adult men, and girls married and began having children.

Role of Elders

Elders were held in high regard in Plateau tribes and performed tasks vital to the survival of tribal culture. In fact, the largest influences in the lives of Plateau children were their grandparents and tribal elders, because they were largely responsible for watching and edu-

Plateau parents loved their children and encouraged them to succeed in the roles reserved for their gender.

cating children in the customs and beliefs of the tribe while parents were away fishing, hunting, and gathering.

When the Lewis and Clark expedition visited the Yakima tribe, Lewis noted a prime example of the respect offered Plateau elders. This report, from his diaries, can be found on the Yakima website: "Those people respect the aged with Veneration. I observed an old woman in one of the Lodges which I entered, She was entirely blind as I was informed by signs, had lived more than 100 winters, She occupied the best position in the house, and when She Spoke great attention was paid to what she Said."[12]

Tribal Organization

The word *tribe* is often used to describe a group of followers of a single chief or council of leaders. The social and political organization of the Plateau people does not fit this description. Rather, Plateau tribes were large groups of family bands that had separate winter camps within the same general area, shared a common territory, and spoke a common dialect. For example, the group of people called the Spokane comprised on average seven thousand people in sixty to seventy semipermanent villages along the Columbia River.

The bands themselves could number anywhere between about twenty and three hundred people, and each family band had its own headman, or spokesman, to represent the group in council with headmen from other bands. This person, however, had little authority over members of the group, relying instead on his powers of

The Indian Grandmother's Role

A native of the Confederated Tribes of the Umatilla Indian Reservation, Esther Lewis tells a story about the role that grandmothers played in the tribe. The story recounted here has been excerpted from the *Indian Curriculum Materials Teacher's Manual, Grades 2–4: The Culture and History of the Cayuse, Umatilla, and Walla Walla Tribes*. The story emphasizes the respect children had for their elders to reinforce the same kind of obedience from tribal children today.

"The grandmother usually stayed in camp while the mother went out into the hills to dig roots, couse and other kinds when the season was right. It was up to the grandmother to care for the children. Families were usually large so there was a number to care for. The grandmother was a very kind and gentle person. She knew what to do if a child was sick or got hurt. She saw to it that they had plenty of good food and took care of their clothing, and made new ones when needed.

When the hunters brought in deer, she helped take care of the meat. She also made the hides into the softest leather to be used for clothing.

Another thing she did in the fall of the year was to go to marshy places where tules grew. Tules are a long reed, when dried, were sewn together into mats [Tuqu]. These mats were used for shelters, to sleep on and make shade while the women worked outside.

The best time of the day was when they went to bed. You know the homes of the people in those days were a circular dwelling, so everyone was in one room. The grandmother told the children stories. This they never hated because that was the time the grandmothers told them their favorite legends and sometimes scary true stories. One favorite was about a mother who had been out in the hills digging roots and gathering berries:

'When the mother came home, she was dry, tired and warm. As she sat down, she asked for some water to drink and wash with. No one brought it to her, they went on playing. She called again, still no one came, so she stood up and in a loud cry called for the Raven to come for her. The Raven came and took her out to the tops of the lodge. She had turned into a bird.

'The children cried and called to the mother to come back, promising to have water waiting for her. Sometime later, the mother returned and true to their promise, there was always water ready for her.

'So, always do what your mother asks!'"

persuasion and on a strong cultural tradition of decision making by consensus. In fact, if an individual or even a headman disagreed with the consensus of the group, he had to either adapt to the wishes of the group or move out of the group.

This informal, somewhat democratic, group-driven system favored among the various tribes of the Plateau proved difficult for Europeans and, later, Americans to understand. When white people came to the region, they wanted a single chief of a large tribe to make all decisions for every band that shared their name without having to consult with anyone else.

Only in times of emergency such as war did a headman or chief take charge of an entire tribe. In such cases, the people of the various bands decided to convene emergency councils at which war leaders were chosen. The members of each band then usually followed the decisions of the leaders their own group had selected. In times of peace, though, these leaders had no more authority than other men in the tribe.

The selection of a headman was seldom based on heredity alone. According to historian and native Spokane David Wynecoop, the Spokane selected a headman "considering the qualities of wisdom, dignity, wealth, warring abilities, and striking physical appearances."[13] Similarly, the Lillooet selected its chief based on his prowess as a fisherman or a hunter. Only the fastest and strongest men and those with a spirit helper became chiefs in bands of Lillooet. Historian Brian Hayden describes these unique skills: "Hunters knew where deer could be found in different seasons and where they would run when approached or wounded. Different informants told me that hunters could close their eyes, see where a deer was fleeing, and tell others where to find it, an ability similar to that of shamans."[14]

Arrival of the Horse

Horses came to be just as important as the physical prowess of humans to a successful hunt. By the early 1800s, traveling from hunting and gathering sites by canoe had become uncommon because of the introduction of the horse. The Sho-shoni had traded the first horses to the Flathead and Nez Percé in the early 1700s. The Shoshoni had gotten their stock from the Comanche, who had stolen them from the Spanish settlements in present-day New Mexico.

Despite the fact that horses were not native to the area, the Plateau's geography provided perfect habitat for them. Its grasslands provided plenty of rich foraging areas. Also, the area's natural boundaries of forests, mountains, rivers, and gorges allowed the Plateau tribes to manage large herds.

At first, horses seemed strange to the Plateau people. In his book *The Native Americans*, historian Colin F. Taylor cites a quote from an Okanagan man discussing his band's awkward first experiences with the horse: "The first horse [we] obtained was very gentle. The first person who mounted it rode with two long sticks, one

After horses were introduced to the Plateau Indians during the 1700s, tribe members quickly became skilled handlers and breeders.

in each hand to steady himself. Another man led the horse slowly, and the rider shifted the sticks as they went along."[15]

Though the horses initially seemed strange, the Plateau Indians quickly became excellent handlers and breeders. So skillful did they become at breeding horses that when Lewis and Clark passed through southeastern Washington and

northeastern Oregon, they found great herds of horses grazing in the foothills.

The Nez Percé had their own breed of horse, one highly sought after by other Plateau Indians, Plains tribes, and whites as well. At first, the Nez Percé had favored white horses, which they painted in bright colors to frighten the enemy as they rode into battle. Soon they began to

Boats of the Plateau

Before the 1700s, all Plateau bands traveled to and from hunting, fishing and gathering, and trade sites in fleets of boats. However, each culture had a special type of boat that distinguished it from another. The Interior Salish tribes of the Thompson, Okanagan, and Shuswap used pointed-front, "sharp-snouted" fish-shaped canoes made of cedar bark. The Coeur d'Alene and Kootenai used rafts made of the same mats they used as walls for their lodges, but they were rolled up, tied together, and shaped into a point at both ends. The Flathead used canoes dug out of logs they hollowed out with fire. Called by the Crow the "A-per-pe," or "the ones who paddle," the Nez Percé made impressive canoes that could be as long as forty feet.

To gather and hunt for food, the Plateau tribes used both rafts and canoes.

Increased contact with other tribes influenced the Plateau Indians' diet, dress, and choice of housing.

develop the speckled Appaloosa. In addition to its distinctive coloring, this breed was faster, larger, and fiercer in battle. Surefooted on dangerous mountain trails, the Appaloosa also could endure trips of longer distances than other breeds. The Nez Percé became known for their highly decorative saddles, pommels, beaded pendants, and halters.

Horse Revolutionizes Plateau Culture

Not surprisingly, the horse revolutionized the lives of the Plateau Indians. Because riding on horses allowed them much greater freedom of movement, they could travel farther and farther from the lowlands of the Columbia River to the upper reaches of distant peaks to gather wild foods and to more easily reach distant trade fairs. On horseback, people could travel up to seventy miles a day—a much greater distance than they could cover on foot.

This increased ability to travel into foreign territories led to increased interactions between the tribes and to the adoption of many new concepts and practices by the Plateau culture. Some eastern groups, such as the Nez Percé, even crossed the Rocky Mountains, riding on horseback to the Plains, where they could kill their own buffalo. They also traded dried roots and salmon with the Crow and Blackfoot for buffalo meat and hides. During their time with the Plains Indians, Plateau people learned how to make tepees, highly portable dwellings that were easy to carry and assemble on long trips. Depending on their success as hunters and traders, they sometimes even used buffalo hides to cover the tepee frames, although tule mat walls remained more common.

Another traveling item borrowed from the Plains Indians was the travois. A travois consists of two long poles tied together with bundles laid across and is pulled along by a horse. This was how Plateau people began carrying their heavy bundles of clothing and supplies on their hunting and gathering trips.

With this increased contact with the Plains Indians came changes in Plateau clothing as well. Wearing traditional clothing made from cloth of shredded plant fibers became less and less common. Instead, people began to wear more buckskin and breechcloths that they had gotten in trade with Plains Indians. Heavily feathered Plains warbonnets also came into style. And on hunting and gathering trips, the Plateau people began wearing parfleches, or hide sacks with drawstrings, instead of carrying traditional bark or woven grass containers.

Tribal Raiding and Skirmishes

The horse was also a catalyst for occasional troubles among the various Plateau cultures. It directly caused a rise in theft. For example, the Spokane raided the Yakima to the south, sweeping in quickly on horseback. In turn, Spokane parties occasionally raided coastal bands to the west and as far south as the Willamette Valley in Oregon. Raiding parties usually stole horses and women for slaves; food and stockpiled weapons were also prime booty. Aside from these occasional raids, however, the Plateau tribes' territories remained fairly intact, so conflict was kept to a minimum.

This time of relative peace began to change when Plateau tribes began making frequent rather than occasional hunting trips into the Plains. While the Plateau groups viewed these areas as part of their legitimate territory, the Blackfoot and the Crow viewed the Plateau Indians' presence as an encroachment upon their hunting grounds. Alternately, the Blackfoot and Crow continued to move closer and closer into Plateau territory and to claim the area as their own. David Thompson, an employee of the Northwest Fur Trading Company, reported in 1787 that "all these Plains, which are now the hunting ground of the above Indians [Blackfoot] were formerly in full possession of the Kootenaes [sic], northward; the next the Saleesh [sic] and their Indians."[16] The Blackfoot regularly forced the Shoshoni, Kootenai, and Flatheads out of what they believed to be their hunting grounds. The problem became so serious that some bands east of the Rockies were all but eliminated by the Blackfoot.

By the early 1800s, these attacks by Plains tribes fueled and strengthened the interdependence among Plateau tribes and helped them create a war complex. The Coeur d'Alene, Flathead, Spokane, Kalispell, Pend d'Oreille, and Nez Percé traveled together in expeditions in areas taken over by Crow and Blackfoot and proved a formidable force. Sometimes the Plains and Plateau tribes declared truces so they could trade necessary items. During an agreed-upon number of days, all of the Indians would consent not to steal horses or fight.

These conflicts arose not out of a hatred for neighboring Indian cultures but out of a serious struggle to supply adequate resources for individual bands. This arduous pursuit of game involved much rigorous preparation, both physical and spiritual. Like other Native American cultures, the Plateau people had a spiritual relationship to the land, which provided them with the food they needed to survive.

Chapter 3

Plateau Spiritual Life

As with many other Native American cultures, the Plateau people's spiritual life revolved around the natural world. This is not surprising, since they made all their clothing, utensils, housing, and food from the natural things they found around them. For example, Plateau people believed that in eating salmon and drinking water from the region, they were communing with its creator. They believed in two supreme beings: Father Sun and Mother Earth.

A religious ceremony common to most Plateau tribes commemorated the seasonal harvests of animals and plants. These events were generally called first food ceremonies. The Umatilla, Cayuse, and Walla Walla tribes celebrated a variation called a Root Feast to express gratitude for the plants, such as camas and bitterroot, they were able to harvest. Similarly, the Flathead celebrated a First Roots Dance, offering songs and prayers that the tribe would have a good harvest. They also held a First Bison Ceremony. The Lillooet people celebrated a First Salmon Ceremony.

The tradition of prayer, singing, dancing, and expressing gratitude to the earth in ancient Plateau food gathering and fishing areas continues today in the form of powwows, events that generally begin in June and end in September.

Creation Stories

The spiritual stories of the Plateau tribes also centered on nature themes. During the long winter months when food and energy had to be conserved, the people spent much quiet time carrying on the tradition of oral storytelling. The elders were the storytellers because of their experience and wisdom. Though their stories were entertaining, that was not the sole purpose for telling them. Each one taught younger members of the group lessons about how to act and about how the creatures around them came into being. Many told of a time before the Indian people existed, when animals could talk and had magical powers. In the Yakima tribe, all stories began with a phrase meaning "This is the way it was

First Fruits Ceremony

Kate McBeth, Presbyterian missionary to the Nez Percé, wrote a book called *The Nez Percés Since Lewis and Clark*. In a reprint of the book with an introduction by historians Peter Iverson and Elizabeth James, McBeth recounts her life among the tribe. The following description offers an intimate look at the Nez Percé's first fruits ceremony.

"The mother earth shared in the honours with the sun father. Their sun worship was at stated times or feasts, as when the fish (salmon) came up and entered the little streams in the spring, and when the first spring roots (Se-with) were fit to eat. The head chief or priest, would call the people of his group of villages to worship. This was the Feast of First-fruits. No one touched them until this ceremony was over, and the chief or priest received first. The worshippers with bowed heads formed a circle. The priest held up a fish to the sun, turning in the direction the sun appears to move around the earth, all chanting as he turned and turned—'Oh! Father, bless the fish. Oh! Father, bless us.' This was their song. They then dug a hole and placed the fish in it, covering it with earth, chanting, 'Oh! Mother, bless the fish. Oh! Mother, bless us.'"

in the legendary days of the animal world!" The children's traditional response of "Eeee!" signified that the young audience was eager to hear the story. Indeed, landmarks mentioned in age-old Yakima creation stories can be found today in the Columbia Plateau, indicating that the tribe has lived there for centuries.

Importance of Coyote

The main character in Plateau creation stories, the coyote was a very powerful natural force. Called by different names in different Plateau cultures, the coyote was sometimes the fool, sometimes the wise one, and most often the trickster. According to most stories, before people had come to live in the Plateau region, Coyote rid the world of monsters to make it safe for humanity.

In the Nez Percé creation story, Coyote, or Iceye'eye, kills the monster Ilt-swi-tsichs, who lives in the Kamiah Valley of Idaho, eating everything in his path. Even Coyote himself is swallowed up, but uses knives he took with him to kill the monster. Coyote then cuts up the body and throws the pieces around. These pieces become the various Indian cultures. Realizing he has not thrown any pieces into the Kamiah Valley, Coyote squeezes blood from Ilt-swi-tsichs's heart, mixes it with water, and sprinkles it on the valley. From this mixture sprang the Nez Percé people. As this story illustrates, most of the time, Coyote's actions helped the Indians; he is often credited with giving them special skills and knowledge.

In the pit houses of the Interior Salish tribe of the Lillooet, further evidence exists to show the significance of the coyote to the Plateau people. Archaeologists re-cently pieced together a possible answer to the mystery surrounding the remains of coyotes found at the bottom of two large storage pits in a Lillooet village.

Archaeologist and writer Brian Hayden believes that the arrangements of the remains in the pit indicates that coyotes had become accustomed to people, were domesticated, and were then accorded special ritual status by the tribe. Ethnographic

Plateau Indians believed the coyote was a sacred animal because it had created their tribes and given them knowledge and skills.

accounts recorded by Simon Fraser and James Teit, travelers to the region, substantiate this idea. When they passed through the Lillooet area in 1808, they saw that some of the tribe's coyotes were eaten in ritual feasts.

During a religious ceremony called the Turning of the Sun, all the Lillooet

Mythological Origin of Salmon

In his book *A Complex Culture of the British Columbia Plateau*, Brian Hayden includes a traditional story told by a Thompson tribal elder about the origin of the salmon. The most common of the stories told about the first salmon, it illustrates how closely the earth and the spiritual beliefs of the Plateau people were linked.

"It is said that in the beginning, the people were without salmon. They heard that some women living at the mouth of the Fraser River had built a weir which prevented the salmon from swimming upstream. Coyote decided that since he was smarter than anyone else, he would go and get the salmon from these women. When he got to the weir, Coyote transformed himself into a wooden plate and washed up against the weir so that the women would find him when they went to get some fish. 'Oh, look at the plate,' called one of the women, 'let's take it home.'

The next day the women left to dig roots, so Coyote changed back into his original form and ate the remainder of the cooked salmon that the women had put aside. He soon noticed the many containers that were in the room and wondered what was in them. Coyote flung open the lid of one of them and out flew hundreds of flies. They circled about Coyote and then began to fly upstream. The women sensed that something was wrong, but when they returned home, all they found was their new plate. The following day, the women again went root-digging, and again Coyote changed back into his original form. He lifted the lid of a second container. This time, wasps swarmed about Coyote and stung him before they flew upstream.

Again the women returned home, but found only a plate. On the third day that the women went to dig roots, Coyote opened another container. This one contained salmon lice! They crawled all over Coyote and then headed upstream behind the flies and the wasps.

On the fourth day that the women went root-digging, Coyote transformed himself back into his original form. He went down to the river, broke the fish weir, and released the salmon. 'Follow me,' he called out to the salmon. Coyote ran along beside the river as the salmon swam upstream. He called out, speaking in the Thompson language, 'Make your fire! The salmon are coming! The salmon are coming up the river!'

Coyote then distributed salmon to the people all along the Fraser River."

people received the wealth that they believed Coyote brought to the tribe. The bounty included salmon, herbs, venison, salmon oil, salmon flour mixed with oil and dried berries, and roasted lily roots. After the feast, all the uneaten remains of coyotes sacrificed during the ceremony were buried in the storage pit, which had been emptied of its goods during the ceremony.

Guardian Spirits

Coyote was not the only natural thing considered powerful to the Plateau Indians. Many types of natural things served as guardian spirits for individuals throughout their lives. In most cultures, children were sent out to find a spirit helper once they had reached a certain age. At age ten, Nez Percé children went into the wilderness alone on a vision quest to find their "tiwatitmas," or spirit helper, which was often an animal. Once at the sacred site of the quest, the child built a fire, which he or she would keep burning at all times. There the child fasted and prayed for two days, turning to face the sun from its rising to its setting. After returning to the family, the child feasted with the family but did not discuss the vision quest.

The Yakima people called a guardian spirit a "takh" and believed a person would carry his takh's power with him into adulthood. In fact, a person could not attain adult status in the tribe until he or she had found a takh. Yakima youths were taught a song by their guardian spirit, which would later be interpreted and asso-

ciated with symbolic items that the person then carried in a small leather bag called a medicine pouch.

Historian Julie Roy Jeffrey says that like the Yakima and the Nez Percé, "the Cayuse sought to make personal connections with the sacred world. The rituals of connection [focused] on the relationship with the weyekin, or guardian spirit. . . . The spirit could be an animal, a growing thing, even a rock or storm cloud. Whatever it was, the spirit would reveal the taboos or special observances that had to be followed in exchange for spiritual guidance."[17]

Beliefs About Sickness

Just as they believed these guardian spirits could provide them with special power, Plateau people also believed that sickness could be traced back to their absence. Jeffrey says that "if, in later years, an Indian fell ill, the sickness was [interpeted to be] a sign that the guardian spirit had fled because taboos had been neglected or because a powerful person's bad magic had driven it away."[18]

Plateau people believed that many sicknesses resulted from an underlying spiritual disorder. In a culture that arose long before the invention of microscopes permitted the development of the germ theory of disease, the occurrence of sickness or death was often attributed to bad or incorrect behavior, such as killing an animal without following a prescribed ritual. Walking on a sacred area could also cause a person to become ill. The Plateau people believed that handling certain sacred items, called totems—believed to be very powerful and potentially dangerous if touched by someone without permission— could cause a serious illness as well.

Healing Medicine

It was the job of the tribe's medicine man or woman, called "twati" by the Yakima and "tewat" by the Cayuse, to heal spiritual disorders. Symptoms of a spirit sickness included reports that a person had seen un-

pleasant visions or heard strange or evil voices. The medicine man knew how to bring the spirit sickness out of a person. In her book *Converting the West*, Julie Jeffrey quotes missionary Narcissa Whitman's description of the tewat's treatment of a sick person, which was "attended by 'horrible' singing, the beating of sticks, bodily contortions, and 'incoherent' speech."[19] The tewat gave sick people medicines made from roots, leaves, flowers, or fir needles. Historian and native Yakima Clifford

Sweat lodges, dome-shaped structures that held in steam coming off of hot rocks, were thought to purify tribe members and protect them from danger.

Trafzer said in his book *Death Stalks the Yakima* that Yakima medicine men called pain "payuwi" and their medicine "tawt-nuk." Trafzer reports that ethnographers and native Yakima "have identified over seventy-five medicinal plants . . . used for healing. . . . Medicinal plants were used to treat people suffering from fever, colds, diarrhea, blood disorders, headaches, stomach ailments, rheumatism, influenza, spider bites, venereal disease, infection, tuberculosis, pneumonia, worms, coughs, [and] arthritis."[20]

Another powerful healing tool of the Plateau tribes was the sweat lodge. Called "Xwi-ach" by the Yakima, the sweat lodge was considered another guardian spirit who could heal, protect, purify, bestow good luck, and ward off danger. Generally, sweat lodges were dome-shaped structures built beside a river. They were first built out of mud, then covered with mats and lined with fir or cedar boughs. Stones were heated in a fire outside, then put inside on the floor of the sweat lodge, and the entrance sealed off. Once inside, participants poured water on the stones to produce steam. Men and women had separate sweat lodges, which usually held up to four people. Boys of some Plateau tribes built their own sweat lodge sometime in puberty as a sign of their passage to adulthood.

In the Flathead story of the origins of the sweat lodge, Blind Mose Chouteh, elder of the tribe, tells the story of how Coyote helped the Indian people build a sweat lodge because he himself had rested and healed in one after killing the destructive monster Ntuk. In Chouteh's story, the sweat lodge says, "Always when you build me, you must use me often and you will always travel in good health."[21]

Death and the Afterlife

When Plateau Indians did die, their tribes buried them. The Spokane sewed the body in buffalo skins or deerskins or robes and placed it on a scaffold in a tree until the grave could be dug. Lillooet Indians were buried in painted coffins called grave boxes or, if a box was not available, in a grave lined with bark or mats. Indicative of the Nez Percé belief in the sacred, eternal spirit of the Columbia River, the Nez Percé buried their dead outside the village near the river, in new clothes and with the head pointing downstream. After a Yakima Indian's burial, his dwelling was burned down, so people wouldn't have to mourn every time they saw it. After one year, the deceased's possessions were given away to friends and family, and the family was allowed to cease mourning and resume full participation in tribal activities.

Details about the Plateau culture's beliefs about the afterlife are sketchy, but the general conviction was that good people went to a pleasant place not unlike the place where they had lived. Indian agent Peter Ronan described the beliefs of the Flathead Indians about heaven:

In the Early times, the Flatheads believed in the existence of a good and evil spirit. . . . They held that often after death the good Indian went to a

Celito Falls (pictured) on the Columbia River was one of several places the Plateau Indians deemed sacred.

country in which there was perpetual summer. . . . The bad man, they believed, would go to a place covered with eternal snow, that he would always be shivering with cold, and would see fires at a distance which he could not enjoy.[22]

Sacred Earth

For Plateau people, certain physical places were considered sacred, and they held their ceremonies there. As historians Arlene Hirschfelder and Martha Kreipe de Montaño explain in the *Native American Almanac:*

Traditional religious practices are inseparably bound to natural formations. Since time immemorial, Indian religious practitioners have gone into sacred high places, lakes, and isolated sanctuaries to pray, fast, make vision quests or pilgrimages, receive guidance, and train young people in the spiritual life of their community. In these sacred places, native people relate to ancestors, humans, plants, animals, and especially to spirits that most often reveal themselves there.[23]

For the Umatilla, Nez Percé, and Warm Springs tribes, Celilo Falls on the Columbia River was an ancient sacred place and frequented until it was flooded to build The Dalles Dam in 1957. Similarly, for the Yakima, Mount Adams in Washington was a sacred site, a place for vision quests and ceremonies.

Like the white missionaries who would come to the Northwest in the nineteenth century, Plateau people had traditional spiritual beliefs, which were expressed in religious observances and worship services. For example, the Yakima's religion, called "Waashat," or the Seven Drum Religion, was distinct from beliefs about guardian spirits and medicine people. Waashat required faith in the creator and prayer. Services were held in the mat lodge of the headman until the mid-1800s when a longhouse was built especially for this purpose. Worship focused on dancing and drumming. The worship leader, called a song counter, held a brass bell to beat out time for the dance. Between songs, elders spoke about things important for the children to remember. As a part of Waashat, a dinner was usually held as well. The worship leader tolled a bell indicating when the people should drink water, which, since they depended upon it for their survival, had religious significance for them.

Christianity Comes to the Plateau Region

Early in the 1800s, Plateau Indians began to come into contact with white Europeans and their religion. During the

The Potlatch

For the Interior Salish tribes of British Columbia, such as the Lillooet, Thompson, and Shuswap, the potlatch was an important ceremony and celebration of nature's bounty. During a potlatch, gifts of meat were given from one person or family to another, increasing the giver's prestige in the tribe. Potlatches were held to honor the dead, to commemorate the naming of children with ancestral names, or to increase the host's prestige.

During the potlatch, the hunting chief, the man with the highest prestige in Lillooet society, distributed the dried or smoked deer meat to all in attendance, even the young, the old, and the sick, who could not contribute gifts of their own.

After contact with other cultures, the potlatch changed forever. As Chinese laborers made their way into towns in the Northwest, their manufactured goods began to turn up in Salish potlatch ceremonies. With the establishment of reservations in the late 1800s and the increasing influence of Catholicism over the people, Christmas feasts replaced the potlatch.

years 1805–1806, Meriwether Lewis and William Clark visited the Plateau region, bringing with them the written word— one primary book being the Bible. The Flathead, Yakima, and Coeur d'Alene heard about Christianity also from members of Iroquois hunting bands who had earlier converted to Catholicism. The Spokane learned about Christianity from Iroquois employees of the Northwest Fur Trading Company in Canada. Initially, the Indians were impressed by the power of the white man's written word to teach and influence.

In the hope that their children could be instructed in the written language, two tribal leaders, Nicholas Garry of the Spokane and J. H. Pelly of the Flathead tribe, agreed to send their children away for Christian instruction. In 1825, Alexander Ross, chief trader at Spokane House, a European trading post, sent Garry's and Pelly's sons to the Episcopal mission at Red River for Christian instruction, where, in five years, they learned to read and write both French and English. These boys returned not only as teachers of the written word but also as preachers of the Christian gospel. As historians Peter Iverson and Elizabeth James write in their introduction to Presbyterian missionary Kate McBeth's account *The Nez Percés Since Lewis and Clark*, the ultimate appeal of Nicholas Garry's son Spokane Garry to the Nez Percé and other Plateau people was not his strict religious teachings but his "remarkable gift of reading and writing."[24]

It was because they wanted to acquire the power they saw in Spokane Garry that in 1831, four Plateau Indian leaders set out on a two-thousand-mile journey to Meriwether Lewis's home in St. Louis to enlist his help in obtaining a copy of the Bible and encouraging white teachers to come back with them. Making up the delegation were the following men: Black or Speaking Eagle (a Nez Percé), Man of the Morning or Daylight (part Flathead, part Nez Percé), Rabbit-Skin-Leggins (part Palouse, part Nez Percé), and No Horns on His Head (Nez Percé).

A Flood of Missionaries

Throughout the first half of the nineteenth century, Catholics, Jesuits, and

In 1831, four Plateau Indian leaders traveled to Meriwether Lewis's (pictured) home hoping he would encourage white teachers to educate Plateau children.

many Protestant denominations, such as Methodists, Presbyterians, and Dutch Reform, sent missionaries to the Plateau region in response to the delegation's message that the Plateau people were interested in the Bible.

This interest arose primarily out of a desire to obtain the power and prestige associated with the ability to read and write, not out of a desire to convert to a new religion. The Plateau delegation did not know that their requests would lead to a flood of missionaries and, consequently, drastic changes in the lives of all Plateau people.

Historians Ken Burns and Dayton Duncan said of the 1831 delegation, "Even after their trip was interpreted by church newspapers as a plea for spiritual salvation, . . . [they] welcomed Protestant missionaries who came west to tell them they had to abandon the ways of their forefathers."[25]

The 1800s brought an increasing number of not only missionaries but also white explorers, hunters, trappers, and traders traveling across the Plateau territory and even settling into the area. With this steady influx of people, fundamental changes in the Plateau culture became inevitable.

Chapter 4

Early Interactions with Whites

Among the first whites to pass through Plateau Indian territory were Meriwether Lewis and William Clark, who had been commissioned by President Thomas Jefferson to explore a land route to the Pacific. Despite some initial and short-lived distrust from the Indians, Lewis and Clark and their crew, called the Corps of Discovery, were well received. The presence of Sacajawea, a Native American guide, calmed the Indians. So friendly was the Flathead early treatment of the Lewis and Clark expedition, for example, that according to Indian agent Peter Ronan in the late 1800s, at the height of tensions between the Flathead and the government, "the new state of Montana, as well as the United States government should not forget that they owe a debt of gratitude to the Flathead Indians for the friendly welcome extended to the early explorers and pioneers of this country."[26]

Tribes Assist Lewis and Clark

Lewis and Clark did indeed depend heavily on the assistance from the tribes of the Plateau. By the time they reached Nez Percé territory, the expedition had been surviving for days on nothing but bear grease and tallow, animal fats used to make candles. They were not only hungry but also tired and sick. When Lewis and Clark wandered into the territory of Nez Percé leader Twisted Hair and his band, the Indians had some difficult decisions to make. Historians Ken Burns and Dayton Duncan said that "according to the tribe's oral traditions, some of the Nez Percé proposed killing the white men and confiscating their boxes of manufactured goods and weapons. The expedition's rifles and ammunition in particular, would have instantly made the Nez Percé the region's richest and most powerful tribe."[27] However, an old woman named Watkweis, or Returned from a Faraway Country, who after being kidnapped by another tribe had been protected and befriended by white Canadians, insisted that the band extend kindness to the explorers.

The trust between the Nez Percé and the members of the expedition built over time. When they left the camp to continue their journey, Lewis and Clark left many goods and horses they could not take with them. When they returned to the Nez Percé band led by Twisted Hair, they received all the goods they had left with the Nez Percé in the fall, and their horses, too, looked healthy, despite a harsh winter that had threatened the health and supplies of the Nez Percé themselves.

News of Visit Spurs Migration

Spurred on further by news of the Corps of Discovery's visit to the Plateau region, French, English, and American traders and trappers poured into the country, eager to profit from the region's riches. These men had few conflicts with the Plateau people. Their success in trapping in the area led to the founding of several trade houses. The Pacific Fur Company was founded at Fort Astoria in 1811 and began competing with the Plateau tribes for food and natural resources.

Despite the potential conflicts, the journals and letters of these trappers describe the Plateau tribes as friendly, helpful, and peaceful. To ensure that relations with the Indians remained peaceful, however, the trading companies did not encourage whites to live in Plateau territory. Any conflicts that developed between the Indians and the white traders were usually resolved by whites giving the Indians the goods that they desired.

Two of the first whites to travel through Plateau territory, Meriwether Lewis and William Clark (standing right) developed a good relationship with the Indians.

Lewis and Clark Visit the Yakima

During the Corps of Discovery, Lewis and Clark traveled the Snake River, reaching the Columbia River and Yakima territory in October 1805. As the Yakima tribal website states, Clark's journal entries "provide a window into a Columbia Plateau tribe." The text, included in the book *The Journals of Lewis and Clark*, edited by Bernard DeVoto, is included here in as near a form as possible as that written by Clark.

"October 16, WEDNESDAY 1805

We halted above the point on the river Kimooenim [Snake] to smoke with the Indians who had collected there in great numbers to view us, here we met our 2 Chiefs who left us two days ago and proceeded on to this place to inform those bands of our approach and friendly intentions towards ail nations &c. we also met the 2 men who had passed us Several days ago on horseback, one of them we observed was a man of great influence with those Indians, harranged them; after Smokeing with the Indians who had collected to view us we formed a camp at the point near which place I saw a hew pieces of Drift wood after we had our camp fixed and fires made, a Chief came from this camp which was about * of a mile up the Columbia river at the head of about 200 men singing and beeting on their drums Stick and keeping time to the musik they formed a half circle around us and Sung for Some time, we gave them all Smoke, and Spoke to their Chief as well as we could by signs informing them of our friendly disposition to all nations, and our joy in Seeing those of our Children around us, Gave the principal chief a large Medal, Shirt and Handkf. a 2nd Chief a Meadel of Small size, and to the Chief who came down from the upper villages a Small Medal & Handkerchief.

The Chiefs then returned with the men to their camp; Soon after we purchased for our Provisions Seven Dogs, Some fiew of those people made us presents of fish and Several returned and delayed with us untill bedtime. The 2 old chiefs who accompanied us from the head of the river precured us Some full Such as the Stalks of weed[s] or plant[s] and willow bushes. one man made me a present of about 20 Ib. of verry fat Dried horse meat."

"October 18th, FRIDAY 1805

The fish being very bad those which was offerd to us we had every reason to believe was taken up on the shore dead we thought proper not to purchase any, we purchased forty dogs for which we gave articles of little value, such as beeds, bells & thimbles, of which they appeared verry fond, at 4 oClock we set out down the Great Columbia."

After fur traders established themselves in the area, Plateau Indians began acquiring their blankets, metal pots, and guns.

A Thriving Plateau Marketplace

Throughout the early part of the nineteenth century, the Northwest Fur Trading Company, a British-owned business, dominated the burgeoning trade by establishing four powerful depots: Kalispell House, Kootenay House, Salish House, and Spokane House. In just a few years of operation, Spokane House would become the predominant trading house in the region.

Obtaining goods from trading houses further changed the lives of the Plateau peoples. Blankets began to be used in place of animal robes. Guns replaced traditional weapons like the bow and arrow. Plateau people even began to cook in metal pots instead of the baskets made of coiled plant roots and other traditional containers.

In some cases, trading even began to change the way Plateau tribes got their food. For example, in 1840, Kamiakin, a Yakima headman, traded horses for cattle from the Hudson's Bay Company, which resulted in the tribe's first herd of longhorns. Before long, beef became a staple in the Yakima diet. Other Plateau tribes

Spokane House: A Fur Trading Center

Founded in 1809 and situated where the Little Spokane flows into the Spokane River, Spokane House became the largest fur trading company in the Columbia Plateau, drawing traders, fur trappers, and Indians from miles around.

The following account, written by trapper Alexander Ross, and included in David Wynecoop's *Children of the Sun: A History of the Spokane Indians*, describes the trading center in its heyday.

"There was a ball room, and no females in the land so fair to look upon as the nymphs of Spokane. No damsel could dance so gracefully as they; none were so attractive. But Spokane House was not celebrated for fine women only, there were fine horses also. The race ground was admired, and the pleasures of the race. Altogether, Spokane House was a delightful place and time had confirmed its celebrity."

While Spokane House basked in its fame and enjoyed the pleasures of the ballroom and the racetrack, a rival firm soon entered the area to compete with it. This was John Jacob Astor's American firm called the Pacific Fur Company. One of Astor's traders, a former Northwesterner named John Clarke, established himself at the corner of the opposition post, then went about winning the Spokane to his own cause. The Indians were assembled, long speeches were made, and mighty things were promised on both sides. As soon as Clarke had got himself settled, he organized outposts, the most notable being one on Coeur d'Alene Lake, where the Spokane River has its origin. For a time it appeared that the new rival would take over the area's trade. However, one year after its construction, because of the war between the United States and Great Britain, the American trading posts were sold to the Canadian firm.

During one season, more than nine thousand beaver pelts were traded in the Spokane district, which included the Snake River, Kootenai River, and Flathead River.

also began planting gardens with seeds purchased at trading houses.

All things considered, the fur companies had a better relationship with the natives than the U.S. government ever would. Little else changed between whites and Indians in the Plateau region until the arrival of the missionaries, which, as historian David Wynecoop writes in his history of the Spokane Indians, "had a more lasting influence than even the white man's guns."[28]

Missionary Influx

Spurred on by accounts of the Plateau Indians' interest in Christianity, missionaries began preparing themselves for life in a new place and moving west. In 1838, one of the first missionaries to the area, Methodist leader Nathaniel Wyeth, established a mission at the heart of Plateau territory, in the Willamette Valley at The Dalles, the Indian trading center. From such a key location, Wyeth had contact with many Plateau cultures who gathered for seasonal trade fairs.

Peter DeSmet, a Belgian-born Jesuit priest, also had a great deal of influence over several tribes. In 1840, he met with Flathead and Pend d'Oreille chiefs, promising to send them a priest. Shortly after, DeSmet and Father Nicholas Point

Peter DeSmet showed Plateau tribes how to plant potatoes and wheat, build semipermanent homes, and raise herds of cattle and hogs.

established St. Mary's Mission in the Bitterroot Valley of Montana to work with the Flatheads and Pend d'Oreille. Some Flatheads even lived in dwellings around the mission with DeSmet, who taught them how to plant wheat and potatoes.

Word spread among the tribes about DeSmet and his work. In 1842, the Coeur d'Alene sent scouts to the Bitterroot Valley to ask DeSmet for priests and teachers as well. DeSmet and his fellow Jesuits had a large impact on the Coeur d'Alene culture. By 1848, families from bands all across Coeur d'Alene territory came to winter in the area near the Sacred Heart Mission at Cataldo, Idaho, and built semipermanent longhouses, giving up their tepees for all but hunting trips. Also, after being instructed by the priests about modern methods of animal husbandry, they also gradually established herds of cattle and hogs instead of putting as much energy and time into hunting and gathering.

The Unsuccessful Spalding Mission

Although in the early days, the Plateau people generally welcomed Christian missionaries with interest and courtesy, DeSmet and his fellow Jesuits were among the few to have had a lasting, positive influence. The disastrous failure of the mission of the Reverend and Mrs. Henry Spalding, sent by the Presbyterian Church in 1836 to establish a mission to the Nez Percé in Lapwai, Idaho, was far more typical. Initially, the Nez Percé were quite impressed with the missionary couple. Mrs.

Spalding learned Sahaptin, the Nez Pecé language, translating her own prayers into their language and establishing a Sahaptin alphabet. Under Mrs. Spalding's tutelage, the Nez Percé also learned English and to read the Bible.

The Spaldings tried, without much success, to get the Nez Percé to convert to Christianity and to alter their customs so that they matched the more stable agrarian lives of whites. They tried to keep Nez Percé boys inside learning the Bible instead of gathering camas during the long and crucial harvest months in the spring and fall. Likewise, they encouraged Nez Percé men to grow gardens instead of leaving the village to fish and hunt. Using tactics typical of many nineteenth-century missionaries, Henry Spalding challenged native beliefs as evil and whipped those who would not convert.

Surprisingly, the Spaldings did see small success in their work with the Nez Percé. Two of the people Henry Spalding finally persuaded to convert and be baptized were Wallowa Nez Percé leader Tuekokas and his wife. Tuekokas, who after baptism took the Christian name Joseph, was the father of Chief Joseph, who would, along with the rest of the Nez Percé people, eventually reject Christianity entirely.

Ultimately, the Spaldings endangered the lives of the people they had come to help and provoked all of the Nez Percé to anger. The winter of 1846–47 was very severe, and families who had obeyed the Spaldings by planting small gardens and studying the Bible instead of participating in the seasonal hunting and gathering trips became completely dependent on the missionaries for food. The Spaldings barely had enough food for themselves, however, let alone enough for the Nez Percé who had been persuaded to stay in Lapwai instead of collecting camas. The whites at the Spalding Mission survived by eating horses, but the Nez Percé refused because the horse was sacred to them. By the summer of 1847, the Nez Percé insisted that the Spaldings leave. When they refused, the Nez Percé destroyed mission property such as windows, the dam, and fences. Finally, Spalding and his wife were chased off the mission property.

Misunderstanding and Bloodshed Mar the Whitman Mission

The story of Marcus and Narcissa Whitman's disastrous ministry was strikingly similar to that of the Spaldings, their friends and fellow Presbyterians. Both the Whitmans had been groomed by strict religious parents to travel to the mission field. Marcus Whitman studied to become a doctor and planned to offer the Indians medical as well as spiritual care. His wife, Narcissa, like other young women in the first part of the nineteenth century, was encouraged to go into missionary work by an inflammatory ad in the *Missionary Herald* newspaper: "SIX HUNDRED MILLIONS OF HEATHENS . . . miserable, and perishing in sin . . . [require] immediate help."[29] In 1838, the couple married and

Although Marcus Whitman treated the Cayuse for measles, the Indians felt his modern medicine caused the disease.

Despite her good intentions, Narcissa Whitman arrived in the West burdened by a set of prejudices that would prove fatal for many, including herself and her husband. Historian Julie Roy Jeffrey includes the following optimistic journal entry that Narcissa wrote at Hudson's Bay Company before they began their work: "Surely my heart is ready to leap for joy, at the thought of being so near the long desired work of reaching the benighted ones and knowledge of a Savior."[30] Narcissa quickly discovered, however, that she did not like working with the Indians as well as she had thought she would. She had difficulty learning the Cayuse language, and because she never came to understand their culture, the Cayuse consistently disappointed her. When they did not respond to the Christian gospel, Narcissa decided that the Cayuse were "proud, vain and frivolous."[31]

When the measles epidemic of 1847 hit the area, the Cayuse's dislike of the Whitmans began to turn into distrust of their unfamiliar medicines. Though Marcus treated the Cayuse with modern medicines, hundreds died. According to historians Robert Ruby and John Brown, rumors circulated among the Cayuse and neighboring Plateau tribes that Marcus Whitman had come to the mission "with a special germ-filled bottle from which . . . he spread measles among them."[32] They

traveled to the Hudson's Bay Company trading post in Vancouver to gather supplies. From there, they went on to establish the Waiilatpu Mission to the Cayuse near the present-day city of Walla Walla, Washington. The Cayuse people were fierce and strong. Having intermarried with the neighboring Nez Percé, they had become excellent horse breeders in their own right, earning a reputation for their stock among both Indians and fur traders. The Whitmans, however, never learned to appreciate the culture and abilities of the Cayuse, who in turn found the missionaries' attitude offensive.

believed this because a white man at the Pacific Fur Company had threatened Indians with just such a vial. Although the rumor about the medicines was false, everyday contact with whites was, in fact,

the source of the measles that infected so many Plateau Indians.

The tensions between the Cayuse and the missionaries finally erupted in violence. Some members of the Cayuse

Fearing that Marcus Whitman wanted to eradicate the entire Cayuse tribe, a group of Cayuse killed Whitman and his wife, Narcissa.

tribe held Whitman responsible for the measles deaths, fearing that he wished to destroy them all. On November 29, 1847, a group of Cayuse stormed the mission kitchen and killed Marcus. In all, fourteen white residents of the mission were killed. Among them was Narcissa, who, before she was killed, was hit in the face with a piece of leather. The Cayuse attackers did not abuse any of the other people they shot. Knowing this, Jeffrey concludes that their treatment of Narcissa "suggests the deep anger they felt at this white woman who had failed to be their friend, who had threatened them with hell, who had held herself . . . apart from them."[33]

The violence did not end with the shootings. The Waiilatpu buildings were burned and forty-seven mission personnel taken hostage. The hostages were taken back to the Cayuse encampment near present-day Mission, Oregon. The fur company at Fort Nez Percé finally secured the return of the survivors, and the Oregon volunteer militia was commissioned to keep the Indians under control. Although the raid had been carried out by only a handful of individuals from a band of Cayuse, the American government and its volunteer army threatened war against all the Plateau Indians unless the perpetrators were turned in. Fearing for the rest of the tribe, a group of Cayuse captured and surrendered the five men responsible for the killings, who were ultimately hanged by the Oregon volunteer militia. Before he was hanged,

one of the men, Tiloukaikt, said, "Did not your missionaries teach us that Christ died to save his people? So die we to save our people."[34]

The Whitmans never converted a single Cayuse to Christianity. Ironically, it was one of the Spaldings' few converts, a Cayuse who lived near their mission, who shot and killed Narcissa. As Jeffrey points out, the Cayuse people would suffer the repercussions of their response to the Whitmans for years to come:

From the vantage point of the twentieth century, the real martyrs would be the Cayuse, who would be punished for their part in the bloody events of 1847 and eventually would experience war, reservation life, and the loss of tribal identity. These would be the unanticipated fruits of the [Whitman's] missionary endeavors at Waiilatpu."[35]

Dreamer Religion

By the time of the Cayuse attack on the mission at Waiilatpu, most Plateau tribes had come to dislike the influence that Christianity had had on their people. The Plateau people and their culture had suffered greatly from the words and actions of Christian missionaries sent supposedly to help them. Many began to follow a Nez Percé spiritual leader called Smoholla, who founded what was called the Dreamer Religion. Smoholla completely rejected Christianity. He preached instead about a kind and loving earth mother who would care for her children in the Plateau and give them wisdom through their dreams. The following is one of Smoholla's renunciations of white ways and beliefs:

> You ask me to plow the ground. Shall I take a knife and tear my mother's breast? . . . You ask me to dig for stone. Shall I dig under her skin for bones? Then when I die I cannot enter her body to be born again. You ask me to cut grass and make hay and sell it and be rich like white men. But how dare I cut off my mother's hair?[36]

Smoholla had a galvanizing effect on the Plateau tribes. Thanks to his influence, many, such as the Nez Percé, would completely reject white ways and religion. They looked increasingly to Smoholla and each other for guidance instead of to the whites who had come to their land and asked them to alter their beliefs and lives in ways they could no longer accept.

As the Indians united against the whites in such ways, however, the conflicts only increased, spelling the end of the relative peace and independence the Plateau tribes had known for centuries.

Chapter 5

Increased White Settlement

In the early 1840s, the British and U.S. governments disputed about who had jurisdiction over the Oregon Territory, which included much of the Plateau region. In 1846, they agreed to split the territory along the Forty-ninth Parallel, leaving Washington, Oregon, Idaho, and western Montana to the United States. This agreement and the consequent opening of the Oregon Trail, a massive land route from Independence, Missouri, to Fort Vancouver, would bring floods of settlers into the Plateau.

The Donation Act

The settlers and the Plateau natives had very different ways of viewing the world. Where the Indians had roamed their territory for generations as hunters and gatherers, settlers lived in permanent settlements and planted crops, rather than eating the plants and animals already living there. Settlers believed that the land they settled on could be claimed solely as their own and that with the construction of fences,

they could keep out all other animals and people.

In 1850, the U.S. Congress passed the Donation Act, which officially permitted whites to claim "unsettled" land in the Plateau region. Under the act, any U.S. citizen could claim up to 320 acres in the Oregon Territory, including lands already occupied by native people. An Indian who wished to obtain land under the Donation Act, had to sever tribal affiliation and become an American citizen. Many Indians refused to accept these conditions and were evicted from land their ancestors had lived on for centuries.

The United States passed additional laws that changed the region. On March 2, 1853, the Oregon Territory was divided into two parts. Washington, northern Idaho, and Montana were designated as Washington Territory. Oregon and southern Idaho became Oregon Territory. That same year, Isaac Stevens was appointed as the first governor of the Washington Territory. Stevens was to simultaneously protect

Believing they had the right to claim any unsettled land, whites from the East flooded the Plateau region via the Oregon Trail.

and safeguard the properties of the settlers in the region and ensure the safety of the Indians already living there—two tasks that on Stevens's watch proved to be mutually exclusive.

As a part of his responsibilities, Governor Stevens was designated as treaty commissioner to enter into agreements with the tribes of the Plateau region, a task for which he was ill prepared. He knew very little about the Indians of the area and did not seek to understand how the whites already living in the area had managed to peacefully coexist with the Plateau people

up to this point. Where the British and Canadians had treated the Indians with politeness and respect, Stevens saw them merely as obstacles to his goal of settling the region.

The Road to the Treaty Councils

Almost immediately after taking office, Stevens sanctioned expeditions into the Plateau region to begin to negotiate with the Indians and acquire land from them. In 1854, a military party led by General George McClellan explored Yakima territory, surveying land where the United States wanted to build a road and railroad line. Indian agent George Gibbs went with McClellan to explain the plan to the Yakima and to encourage them to cede legal title to their territory so that it could be completely opened to white settlement— something the United States planned to ask of all Plateau tribes. Gibbs told tribal leaders that the United States would relocate the Yakima to a reservation.

After talking to the Yakima, Gibbs decided that the plan was a bad one and recommended against encouraging the Yakima or any other Plateau tribe to give up their land. Gibbs expressed concern that considering their hunting and gathering lifestyle, Plateau people could not adapt to life on reservations. He said that they must have the ability to roam, hunt, and collect seasonally to survive. Though General McClellan agreed with Agent Gibbs, Governor Stevens ignored their recommendation.

Feeling increasing pressure from settlers and government officials, Yakima leaders tried to unify the various bands and other Plateau tribes so that they could all better defend themselves. When it became clear that Stevens wanted to take their land from them, Yakima leader Kamiakin called a council in the Grande Ronde Valley to form an intertribal confederacy. As a result of the meeting, the Yakima joined with the Cayuse, Walla Walla, Umatilla, and Nez Percé, forming a united front against any attempts to get them to cede their land.

On May 28, 1855, approximately six thousand Indians from the confederation of Plateau tribes convened in the Walla Walla Valley of Washington for a meeting with Stevens's treaty commission. The Indians rode single file into the valley. Warriors fired their guns, displayed weapons, screamed, and beat their drums to indicate to Stevens that they were strong, well organized, and powerful. A similar council called the Hellgate Council was held with the Pend d'Oreille, Salish, and Kootenai tribes (Flathead). It was an attempt to get the three disparate groups to agree to live in one location, ceding all other land to the U.S. government.

Difficult Negotiations End in Pressure on Tribal Leaders

Treaty negotiations were difficult, particularly because Governor Stevens, who as treaty commissioner was empowered to enter into agreements with the Plateau tribes, was poorly suited to the job. Failing to understand the individual autonomy of local bands of tribes, he named "chiefs" who were to make decisions for the members of their entire tribe. These appointees, in turn, made decisions impacting bands not even represented at the councils.

Most tribal leaders were reluctant to sign the treaty Stevens offered, however, and to move the process forward, the governor pitted the leaders of the different groups against one another. For example, Stevens induced the leaders of the Pend d'Oreille and Kootenai tribes to sign by

Isaac Stevens was assigned to protect both the whites and the Plateau Indians, but he favored the interests of the settlers.

and persuaded him to encourage the others to sign the treaty. Only when it became clear that the tide was turning against them—that they could have a small portion of their existing territory or none at all—did all the other tribal leaders sign the treaty. Most felt that they had never had any choice in the matter and that the treaty's terms had been decided without their input. Moreover, with hindsight, it is clear that many "chiefs" did not understand the legal implications of the document they had signed.

A Flawed Treaty Guarantees Future Problems

The treaty of 1855 rearranged Plateau tribal groups and territory. Reservations were created on the Plateau: one for the Salish and Kootenai (otherwise known as the Flatheads); one for the Walla Walla, Umatilla, and Cayuse; one for the Yakima; and one for the Nez Percé. Only 1 percent of the reservation land bordered the Columbia River, which was so important to the people's survival. New tribal groups were created based on the reservation designations. The U.S. government called the Umatilla, Walla Walla, and Cayuse all by the single name Umatilla. Based purely on geographic closeness, the treaty also lumped together fourteen independent, un-

offering them a deal that would have forced Flathead leader Chief Victor and his entire tribe out of their homeland of the Bitterroot Valley into the Flathead Lake region.

Similarly, when Kamiakin and Walla Walla chief Peupeumoxmox felt pressured into signing the treaty at the Walla Walla council, they asked for a recess. Not to be outmaneuvered, Stevens privately named another, more cooperative Nez Percé leader named Lawyer as chief related tribal bands, calling them the U.S. Consolidated Tribes and Bands of the Yakima Indian Nation.

The 1855 treaty made the Indians extravagant promises that for a variety of reasons, the U.S. government ultimately did not keep. To have kept their promises to all of the tribes would have required a huge financial investment that the government was not prepared to make. Besides monetary compensation, the treaty also promised the construction of reservation schools, blacksmith and gunsmith shops, flour mills, and hospitals. It also promised to send professionals such as carpenters and doctors to help the people on the reservations. Even though the treaty said that no whites would be allowed to live on reservation lands except by Indian permission, the United States consistently failed to honor or enforce parts of the treaty that did not favor white settlers. Also, the treaty granted the Indians permission to hunt and gather on land off the reservation that was not already claimed by settlers—a right that the United States could not provide enough officials to actually defend.

Though Stevens also promised the Plateau people that settlers would obey the boundaries of the reservations set out in the treaty, shortly after its signing, he sent word to newspapers such as the *Puget Sound Courier* and the *Oregon Weekly Times*, announcing the opening of the inland Northwest. The land rush began. White settlers flooded across reservation land, unclear about reservation boundaries.

Treaty Loses Meaning

As tensions increased between Indians and whites, the 1855 treaty became virtually meaningless. Battles broke out in the late 1850s that would eventually lead to war. To complicate matters, volunteer militias that operated independently of U.S. forces joined the fray. With Governor Stevens's blessing, the Oregon Mounted Volunteers under the command of Colonel James Nesmith raided the countryside, stealing food and pillaging from French-Canadian trappers and settlers as well as Indians. Walla Walla chief Peupeumoxmox, in what he thought was a two-sided attempt to achieve a truce with the militia, was captured by Nesmith's men and murdered. The Oregon Mounted Volunteers took pieces of his body as souvenirs of the battle.

In light of these violent events, Governor Stevens's handling of Indian affairs came under criticism. The U.S. commander of the army's department of the Pacific, John Wool, criticized Stevens and refused to escort him through hostile Indian territory. In sharp disagreement with Stevens and the Oregon Mounted Volunteers, Wool maintained that instead of making war with the Indians, the U.S. Army needed simply to police the area, protecting both Indians and settlers until the 1855 treaty could be ratified by the president of the United States.

Tensions Mount

Disagreements about how to solve the problem raged between Stevens and his

U.S. Army commander John Wool disagreed sharply with Isaac Stevens's policy toward the Indians.

volunteer militia and the U.S. Army, aggravating an already confusing and volatile situation. As aggressive white settlement continued into the area, U.S. Army troops were sent to keep settlers out of Plateau territory. Stevens took a different approach. Instead of trying to control the settlers in the area, he sent volunteer troops to battle Plateau people, some of whom had not been involved in the conflict. The tensions increased until Commander Wool ordered the Oregon volunteer forces out of the area and they disbanded. In late 1857, Wool closed the interior Plateau lands to white settlers and tried to make all existing settlers leave. That same year, Stevens resigned his post as territorial governor to take a seat in Congress.

This time of peace on the Plateau was short-lived. In the summer of 1858, gold was discovered on the Thompson and Fraser Rivers in British Columbia. Prospectors crossed onto Indian territory and war broke out again. U.S. Army Colonel E. J. Steptoe was sent from Fort Walla Walla to fight the alliance of Palouse, Coeur d'Alene, Yakima, Spokane, Cayuse, and Walla Walla. The Indian War of 1858 had officially begun.

The Indian War of 1858

Steptoe's efforts to subdue the Indians were hampered because he was unclear about which people belonged to which tribes and which territory was used by each tribe. For example, Steptoe moved into Palouse territory and accused the people of raiding army camps in Walla Walla Valley and of stealing horses. But he stormed through Coeur d'Alene territory as well, thinking it belonged to the Palouse. When informed of his mistake, he claimed to be on a peaceful mission to the Spokane. The Indians questioned why, if he came in peace, so many troops carried so many rifles.

Though they won many battles, the confederacy of Palouse, Coeur d'Alene, Yakima, Spokane, Cayuse, and Walla Walla lost the war. By the end of the conflict, Colonel George Wright's forces exacted a heavy penalty on the retreating Indian confederacy. Wright traveled to Spokane Falls, where he had determined to break their forces. In the final days of the conflict, they met Wright's army near the site of present-day Fairchild Air Force Base but were badly defeated. At Spokane Falls, Wright ordered that Indian horses be slaughtered and dumped into the river rather than kept. This was a serious affront to the Plateau people, who held horses sacred. In addition, Wright ordered troops to move through Spokane territory, destroying food supplies. In September of 1858, Wright drafted a peace treaty for the alliance leaders to sign.

Flathead Railroad Treaty

In 1872, soon to be president but then General James Garfield came to force the Flatheads to the Jocko reservation because the Northern Pacific wanted access to the land to build a railroad. When Chief Charlot and his band refused, the U.S. government demanded they pay taxes on their land in the Bitterroot Valley. Finally in 1891, the conditions became so bad for the members of Charlot's band that he marched them from the Bitterroot Valley to the Jocko reservation. Included in "The Indian and Taxation," an essay in *The Last Best Place: A Montana Anthology*, edited by William Kittridge and Annick Smith, is Chief Charlot's protest:

"Yes, my people, the white man wants us to pay him. He comes in his intent and says we must pay him—pay him for our own, for the things we have from our God and our forefathers for things he never owned and never gave us. What law or right is that? What shame or what charity. . . . Yes they say we are not good! Will he tell his own crimes? No, no; his crimes to us are left untold. . . . His laws never gave us a blade of grass nor a tree, nor a duck, nor a grouse, nor a trout. No; like the wolverine that steals your cache, how often can he come? You know he comes as long as he lives, and takes more and more—and dirties what he leaves."

Nez Percé Cannot Avoid Conflict

Though for the most part, the Nez Percé, the most famous Plateau tribe, stayed out of the war embroiling most of the other tribes, they could not avoid conflict. Settlers daily crossed their territory, stealing their horses and harassing them. Indian agents advised them to let the settlers trespass, saying that they did not want Nez Percé land, but only to cross it. However, in 1860, gold was discovered directly on Nez Percé reservation land beside the Clearwater River in present-day Pierce City, Idaho. As word about gold spread, miners flooded into the area, disregarding the limits the 1855 treaty placed on them. Though the Nez Percé asked for enforcement of the treaty, settlers pressured the government for access to more land in Plateau territory. In response, the Senate appropriated funds in 1862 to reconfigure the reservation, leaving much less land to the Nez Percé.

In 1863, U.S. officials presented a revised treaty they hoped Nez Percé leaders would sign at a treaty council at Lapwai. Nez Percé Chief Joseph refused, however, asking why he should trust the United States to enforce a new treaty when they had not enforced the one written in 1855. Chief Joseph and many Nez Percé leaders said that more than anything else, they could not agree to the reduced size of the reservation. The U.S. government representatives, called Indian agents, responded that having a smaller reservation to patrol

Chief Looking Glass and his Nez Percé tribe could not avoid conflict with white settlers.

would make it easier for U.S. troops to protect the residents, but the Indians were unconvinced.

As with the other Plateau groups, the Nez Percé bands all operated independently of one another—something that the government negotiators did not understand. After days of discussions with the Indian agents, fifty Nez Percé men, including Lawyer, Timothy of Alpowa, and Jason of Asotin, agreed to the terms of the 1863 treaty if they could continue to live in peace on the land outside the new boundaries. But Chief Joseph and the other leaders who felt as he did were furious that the agents based their actions upon the decision of a few rather than the whole. The 1863 treaty left the Nez Percé with just one-tenth of the original reservation. In all, 6,932,270 acres were lost, including the Wallowa Valley, which was the homeland of Chief Joseph's father and one of the few fishing areas left on the reservation for the Nez Percé. The U.S. government paid the Nez Percé eight cents an acre for the land.

Nontreaty Faction Holds Fast

The Lower Nez Percé, called the nontreaty faction and led by Chief Joseph, said they would not agree to the treaty that Lawyer and the others had signed. They called it the "Thief Treaty."

The Nez Percé were not without allies in the U.S. government, however. In the early 1870s, Nez Percé agent John Monteith wanted to set aside the Wallowa Valley for the Nez Percé to use without interference. In response, an 1873 executive order of President Ulysses S. Grant ceded certain lands to the Nez Percé—the lower portion of the valley, an area already occupied by whites.

The error was soon pointed out, but the incorrect boundaries were never redrawn, putting the nontreaty Nez Percé and the whites in direct conflict with each other. Oregon governor Lafayette Grover agreed with white settlers in the state that the nontreaty Nez Percé must be moved onto reservation land in Idaho. The final blow came in 1875, when President Grant rescinded his executive order and said that all Nez Percé must go to the reservation.

By this time, Chief Joseph's band had completely rejected Christianity, and the chief himself had torn up a copy of the New Testament in front of General Oliver Howard. Finally, after days of unsuccessful negotiations, Chief Joseph and the general reached an impasse. Joseph said he would not cede the Wallowa Valley to the government. He said it was not his to sell, that land could not be owned. The council broke down without a resolution, and under threat of military attack, all the nontreaty Nez Percé leaders sadly agreed to move onto the reservation. Because Howard believed that there was potential for serious conflict between Indians and whites, he gave the Nez Percé just thirty days to completely relocate from their home of many generations. On April 1, 1877, the Nez Percé set out on their journey. To reach Idaho, they all—young and old, sick and healthy alike—had to cross the Imnaha River with all their belongings. In spring, the water was very high and dangerous. After this first dangerous leg of their journey toward the reservation, the bands of nontreaty Nez Percé gathered for

A Trip to the National Park

Emma Carpenter Cowan's account of her encounter with the Nez Percé, "A Trip to the National Park in 1877," is anthologized in *The Last Best Place: A Montana Anthology*, edited by William Kittridge and Annick Smith. Cowan and her husband and friends visited the newly established Yellowstone Park. On their way, they encountered Chief Joseph and his band of nontreaty Nez Percé on their exodus to Canada. When Cowan and her party tried to leave the park, forty to fifty Indians followed them, eventually taking all their wagons and supplies and holding them hostage. When he attempted to defend himself and the party, Cowan's husband was shot by the Nez Percé and left for dead. He and the rest of the party were later rescued by the troops of General Oliver Howard, the senior U.S. military officer in the territory.

Despite the experience, Cowan spoke well of the Nez Percé: "Regardless of the fact that they had been harassed and hard pressed and expected battle every moment . . . the majority of the Nez Perces were light-hearted and seemed not to worry over the outcome of their campaign. Perhaps to worry is a prerogative of the white race."

Most interesting are Cowan's impressions of Chief Joseph: "My brother tried to converse with Chief Joseph, but without avail. The chief sat, by the fire, sombre and silent, foreseeing in his gloomy meditations possibly the unhappy ending of his campaign. The 'noble red man' we read of was more nearly impersonated in this Indian than in any I have ever met. Brave and dignified, he looked like a chief."

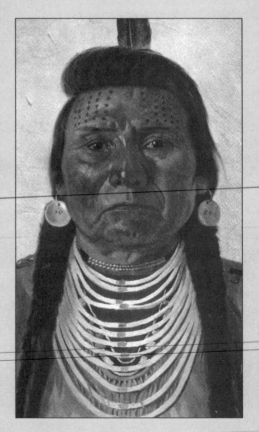

Despite her negative experience with the Nez Percé, Emma Carpenter Cowen called Chief Joseph (pictured) noble, brave, and dignified.

After a summer of battles, Chief Joseph (with arm raised) surrendered to Colonel Nelson Miles and the U.S. Army in 1877.

one last, symbolic time on the Camas Prairie, the ancient site near present-day Grangeville, Idaho, to dig camas and fish for salmon.

Irreversible Violence

At this gathering, a warrior named Wahlitits set out to avenge the death of his father at the hands of a white settler. He and two other Nez Percé warriors raided settlements along the Salmon River, killing a white soldier and three other men. Soon he had persuaded an entire band of Nez Percé warriors to fight settlers they believed were driving them from their homeland. Once they learned of these events, the rest of the Nez Percé knew they would have to fight the now-enraged U.S. forces.

Battles between Nez Percé and the U.S. Army went on throughout the summer of 1877, with the Indians losing many of their finest warriors, as well as noncombatants. Then, with winter aproaching and only a hundred Nez Percé remaining, Chief Joseph met with Colonel Nelson Miles to arrange a surrender.

The Aftermath of Chief Joseph's Surrender

Chief Joseph and other Nez Percé under-stood from Miles that when they surren-dered, they would be allowed to travel in peace to the Nez Percé reservation in Idaho. General William Tecumseh Sher-man, however, reversed Miles's decision, saying that the Nez Percé could not even rest the winter in Montana, but must imme-diately be moved along the Yellowstone and the Missouri Rivers to a reservation in Fort Leavenworth, Kansas. On No-vember 27, 1877, the Nez Percé were loaded onto flatboats and sent to Fort Leavenworth.

By the time of the Nez Percé defeat, most of the Plateau people—even those in British Columbia, Canada, who were under British jurisdiction—had already settled onto reservations. Two holdouts were the Flatheads and the upper and middle bands of the Spokane. Chief Vin-cent, then chief of the Flatheads, insisted on the tribe's rights to remain off the reservation in their ancestral home of the Bitterroot Valley, which was rich with plants and game. He did live in the area near present-day Stevensville until his death in 1870, but by this time he and the other members of his tribe were sur-rounded by white settlements. His son and successor, Charlot, refused to leave as well, but finally in August 1884, the Flathead were all moved to the Jocko reservation in Montana.

Like the Flatheads, the upper and mid-dle bands of Spokane had been reluctant

Chief Joseph's Surrender

On October 4, 1877, Chief Joseph asked Colonel Nelson Miles to relay the follow-ing now-famous words to General Oliver Howard. This excerpt appears in *The Last Best Place*, edited by William Kittridge and Annick Smith:

"I am tired of fighting. Our chiefs are killed. Looking Glass is dead. Toohulhul-sote is dead. The old men are all dead. It is the young men who say yes or no. He who led the young men (Joseph's brother Ollikut) is dead. It is cold and we have no blankets. The little children are freezing to death. My people, some of them, have run away to the hills and have no blan-kets, no food. No one knows where they are—perhaps freezing to death. I want to have time to look for my children and see how many of them I can find. Maybe I shall find them among the dead. Hear me, my chiefs. I am tired. My heart is sick and sad. From where the sun now stands I will fight no more forever."

to move onto the Spokane reservation, which had been established in the territory of the Lower Spokane, because they did not think the land was desirable. Finally in 1887, having been forced out of ancestral tribal fishing and hunting areas by white settlers and unable to survive on what little they could gather, the upper and middle bands agreed to move onto the reservation.

In the final decades of the nineteenth century and the first half of the twentieth, the Plateau people would suffer not only the loss of their land but also their health, pride, and cultural identity.

Chapter 6

Lost Lands, Lost Identity

The years immediately following the Plateau people's removal to reservations were difficult ones. Drastic changes in the Plateau people's diet and lifestyle brought disease, hunger, and poverty. Facing an immensity of practical and financial constraints, the U.S. government failed to follow through on many treaty promises of hospitals, mills, and other buildings and services needed for the Indians to adapt to the new agricultural way of life now thrust upon them. Also, since disparate tribes were now shoehorned into small, shared territories, intratribal conflicts developed.

Cultural Disintegration

One of the first of its promises the U.S. government did follow through on, the education of Indian children, had a largely negative impact on Plateau culture. If they were not sent to schools already operating near their reservation, children were sent away to special Indian boarding schools. In addition to learning English and agricul-

tural skills, the children were taught different ideas and habits that teachers believed would allow them to better assimilate into white culture. Though it was intended to help the Indians adjust to their new lives, taking the responsibility of educating children away from the tribe contributed to the disintegration of the tribal cultures. Without their elders, children no longer had access to information about tribal tasks and traditions and began to become less familiar with their native languages.

One of the most difficult cultural changes of all, Plateau people were not allowed to leave the reservation lands without a government-issued permit. This meant that they could not travel, as a group, to other areas to gather traditional foods such as salmon and roots. During treaty negotiations in 1855, Governor Stevens had indicated that Indians would still have access to ancestral fishing, hunting, and gathering grounds.

In other cases, many ancient fishing and root-gathering grounds were destroyed.

Many dams were constructed on the Columbia River in the early 1900s to provide steady sources of water for burgeoning western towns. Many prime fishing and root-gathering areas were flooded by the rising waters. Celilo Falls, one of the most famous hunting and gathering sites as well as a trade center, is one prime example. Also, settlers in the region drained water from the rivers to irrigate their cropland. This irrigation, coupled with the diversion of huge amounts of water from the Columbia River to fill reservoirs, interfered with seasonal salmon spawning and nearly

After the Plateau Indians moved on to reservations, white settlers took over ancient fishing areas like this one on the Columbia River.

wiped out the once healthy population in the area. Though the U.S. government promised to create hatcheries to restore the dwindling salmon population, they most often did so far from reservation land where Indians were allowed to fish.

If fishing areas were intact, frequently settlers prevented the Plateau Indians' legal access to ancestral fishing ground because they owned the land the Indians needed to cross to reach them. Though the Indians' rights to these areas were upheld in federal court, there was little way to enforce the law. In just one of many legal battles the Plateau people would have to fight to gain access to fishing grounds, Yakima chief George Meninock made the following speech in federal court:

> God created this Indian Country as it was like He spread out a big blanket. He put the Indians on it. . . . Then God created the fish in this river and put deer in these mountains and made laws through which has come the increase of fish and game. . . . When we were created we were given our ground to live on, and from that time these were our rights. This is all true. We had the fish before the missionaries came, before the white man came. . . . This was the food on which we lived. . . . My strength is from the fish; my blood is from the fish, from the roots and berries. The fish and game are the essence of my life. . . . We never thought we would be troubled about these things. . . . Whenever the seasons

open, I raise my heart in thanks to the Creator for His bounty that this food has come.[37]

White Settlements

In the final decades of the nineteenth century, many people came to the Plateau region to take advantage of open space and job opportunities. In addition to whites, immigrants from Asia and Mexico settled in the area, staking claims on the region's now valuable agricultural land. Cut off from fishing and gathering and as yet unskilled in agriculture, many Plateau people resorted to working as day laborers in the fields or as fruit pickers.

Unsettled farmland was fast disappearing. With irrigation and other new techniques of growing crops in the Plateau's often dry soil, it became evident that the reservation lands provided some of the last remaining areas available for farming. As they were put into ever-closer proximity to each other, the Indians and farmers began to have more conflicts. When local attempts to loosen reservation boundaries so that they could be opened to farming failed, settlers became more jealous and resentful of the Indians and agitated for their removal.

Indians were, however, able to take advantage of some of the land legislation enacted. In 1884, the U.S. government enacted the Indian Homestead Act, expanding the Homestead Act of 1862, which said that any U.S. citizen over twenty-one could claim 160 acres of unsettled public land. Under the new legislation, Indians could claim the same amount of land. Though in many instances, settlers tried to convince the U.S. military to force homesteaded Indians back onto reservation land, many were able to hold their ground.

Railroad Lines Built

Though stagecoach lines had been in place for several years, a burst of railroad building in the 1880s brought additional tension to the area. The railroads provided a direct line for supplies, making it far easier for settlers to establish themselves in the Plateau region than if they had had to carry all their supplies and belongings by wagon.

When it came to building railroads, neither the U.S. government nor the railroad companies honored reservation boundaries. One railroad company, the Northern Pacific, claimed a total of fifty-five thousand acres of land within the Spokane reservation. "The railroad," reports David Wynecoop, historian and native Spokane, "said that it was entitled to the land as an incentive for building the railroad to the city of Spokane."[38] The railroad lost its claim, but only after nearly five years of legal battles.

In another case, U.S. government officials pressured Flathead leaders into signing a treaty selling a large portion of the

Railroad companies invaded the Plateau region and disregarded reservation boundaries.

Jocko reservation to the Northern Pacific. The negotiation proceedings illustrate that the Indians well understood what was happening but recognized their ultimate powerlessness. Told by the treaty commissioner that an earlier treaty signed by "their fathers" bound the Flatheads to give up still more land "if necessary for public convenience," Chief Eneas responded, "This reservation is a small country, and yet you want five depots upon it. These are the best parts on the reservation. What are we going to do when you build the road? We have no place to go. That is why it is my wish that you should go down the Missoula River. . . . [T]his is a small country and we are holding on to it like a child to a piece of candy."[39]

Eventually, having been threatened with military action if they refused, the leaders signed the treaty. What the Flathead people feared came true: The railroad went through, bringing with it an additional influx of settlers. The Indians were offered

The Ground Speaks

The Plateau tribes believed that without growing crops or raising livestock, as they would be encouraged to do on the reservations, they could survive off the natural bounty of the earth. Quoted in the Confederated Tribes of the Umatilla Indian Reservation Website, Young Chief of the Umatilla tried to explain this idea to whites who wanted them and the other Plateau tribes to move from their traditional fishing and gathering grounds onto reservations.

"I wonder if the ground has anything to say? I wonder if the ground is listening to what is said? I wonder if the ground would come alive and what is on it? Though I hear what the ground says. The ground says, it is the great spirit that placed me here. The great spirit tells me to take care of the Indians, to feed them alright. The great spirit appointed the roots to feed the Indians on. The water says the same thing. The great spirit directs me, feed the Indians well. The ground, water and grass say, the great spirit has given us our names. We have these names and hold these names. The ground says, the great spirit has placed me here to produce all that grows on me, trees and fruit. The same way the ground says, it was from me man was made. The great spirit, in placing men on the earth, desired them to take good care of the ground and to do each other no harm."

Despite this and many other impassioned pleas from the Plateau people, they were moved onto reservations, and their lives, and the land on which they had lived, changed forever.

sixteen thousand dollars for the large tract of valuable land, and the treaty commissioner told them that they must "depend on his [the President's] judgment as to how the money will be paid."[40] They never received the money.

The General Allotment Act of 1887

The U.S. government finally succumbed to pressure from settlers, railroads, and other people with interest in the Plateau region to open even the reservation lands. Many well-meaning officials believed that if Indians actually owned their land, they would take pride in it and want to raise crops and livestock on it. Senator Henry Davies drew up a plan where reservations would be split into little plots called allotments that would then be given to each Indian family. Any additional land left after the plots had been assigned to the Indians would then be opened up for settlement by non-Indians. In 1887, the General Allotment Act passed Congress. Over the next two decades, all reservation lands were surveyed and a census taken of each tribe. All Indian heads of families were given 160 acres. Title to the land would be held by the government for twenty-five years, during which, people who had received allotments would not be required to pay taxes on them. After the twenty-five years expired, however, title would revert to individual landholders, who would then be responsible for paying taxes on the formerly tax-free acreage.

Many Plateau people had concerns about what the act would mean for them.

They worried that the reservation would no longer be occupied only by Indians and that it would put them in direct contact with settlers, thereby increasing conflict. Many Indians who already maintained large herds of animals on tracts of land larger than the allowed 160 acres understandably opposed the act. The legislation caused conflicts not only between Indians and whites but also between tribal members whose new allotments often crossed land previously owned by another within the tribe. The Plateau people's greatest fear was that the act would open up Indian land for sale again and that they would, when all was said and done, lose even the small reservations set aside for them.

Their fears were justified. Unfamiliar with agricultural practices and unable to purchase equipment or secure irrigation rights, many Plateau families wound up selling their acreage to settlers. Once occupying 3 billion acres of land in the continental United States, the Native Americans had only about 48 million acres by the time the General Allotment Act was repealed in 1934. Those Indians who did stay on their allotments came in ever-closer contact with whites, which increased their exposure to things, such as alcohol, that would begin to degrade their health.

Health Problems

Life on reservations and limited allotments of land changed the Plateau people's lifestyles and, consequently, their health. Perhaps the most striking and detrimental

After moving to reservations, like the Nez Percé Agency (pictured), the Plateau Indians' health deteriorated because they had less access to their usual, healthy foods.

of these changes involved their diet. Because many of the traditional areas for collecting roots and plants had been plowed or flooded, Plateau people could not hunt deer or fish for salmon as easily as they had before the influx of settlers. Without this healthy traditional diet, which had been high in vitamins and fiber and low in saturated fat, they were forced to make less nutritious choices. In his book *Death Stalks the Yakima*, writer and native Spokane Clifford E. Trafzer says, "During the course of the twentieth century, they relied more heavily on processed, refined foods which they purchased with cash or received as government commodities."[41] This poor diet led to an abnormally high incidence of gastrointestinal disorders, diabetes, heart disease, high blood pressure, and other chronic degenerative diseases.

Because they no longer traveled through large territories on seasonal hunting and gathering trips, the Plateau people began to lead more sedentary lives that required less exercise. This also contributed to the higher risk of heart disease and diabetes, diseases often associated with inactivity.

Inadequate housing and facilities on the reservations also contributed to health declines. Reservation houses built for the

Nez Percé and the Reservation

Of all the Plateau peoples, Chief Joseph's band of Nez Percé suffered the most following their move to the reservation. Instead of being permitted to remain in their home region as the other tribes had been allowed to do, this band of Nez Percé was sent to Fort Leavenworth, Kansas, a climate very different from the one they had left. Many died of illnesses brought on by extreme depression or because they could not adapt to the hot, humid, and, to them, inhospitable weather. Also, they were placed on mosquito-ridden river-bottom land, so many came down with malaria.

In July 1878, the tribe was again moved to the Quapau reservation in northeast Oklahoma. Inadequately notified of their arrival, Indian agent William Whitman had not prepared the proper shelters or supplies for them, so many more died of exposure and starvation. The tribe called the reservation the "Eckish Pah," which means "hot place."

Over time, many whites took up the Nez Percé cause. In 1879, Chief Joseph and another leader, Yellow Bull, met with politicians in Washington asking to be allowed to return home, despite lobbying efforts by officials in the Northwest to keep them from returning. That same year, Chief Joseph published an autobiography, and many of the people who read it petitioned the government that the Nez Percé be allowed to return to their homeland.

Finally on April 29, 1885, Commissioner of Indian Affairs John Atkins allowed the Nez Percé to return to Lapwai. However, Chief Joseph and 150 other Nez Percé were sent instead to the reservation in Colville, Washington, because of war crimes committed against the U.S. Army. Of the 431 people originally sent to Leavenworth, only 268 had survived.

In 1900, an aging Chief Joseph asked permission to buy a small piece of land in his homeland of the Wallowa Valley, but his request was denied. He died in 1904.

Following the move to reservations, Chief Joseph's tribe suffered an unfamiliar climate, inadequate housing, and disease.

Poor housing, as pictured here in the Coville Agency, and the lack of a good sewer system contributed to the health problems of the Plateau people.

Indians were poorly ventilated and harbored bacteria. Also, inadequate supplies of clean water and inadequate sanitary sewers created unhygienic conditions on reservations as well.

Medical care on reservations also lagged far behind the rest of the nation. Throughout the late nineteenth and early twentieth centuries, most reservations lacked access to public health programs. They did not have enough doctors, advanced medicines, or hospitals and clinics. The responsibility for the medical care of the Plateau people fell on the U.S. Congress and the Bureau of Indian Affairs, neither of which designated adequate funds for health programs.

Beginnings of Self-Governance

Gradually, Plateau people began to band together to address and take responsibility for some of these and other problems facing them and other Native Americans on the reservations. With the increasing cooperation of the U.S. and Canadian governments, the tribes took on the responsibility of governing themselves. The United States opened the door for this in 1924, passing the Snyder Act, which gave all Native Americans full citizenship and its associated rights. Before this time, Indians could become citizens only by severing their tribal affiliation. In 1934, passage of the Indian Reorganization Act gave Indians the right to practice their own religion without interference and to govern themselves.

As they dealt increasingly with the U.S. government, Plateau tribes adapted their own tribal governments to facilitate future meetings and decision making. In the past, Plateau people had operated under a loose, egalitarian form of governance, appointing chiefs only in times of war or other crisis. But as before, U.S. officials preferred to deal with a few people who could speak for all tribal members. Consequently, as tribes set up their own governments, they leaned more toward governments led by general council or by a board of a small number of tribal leaders elected to speak on behalf of the rest of the tribe and to handle all administrative and legal matters.

Gradually, each tribe drafted and ratified its own constitution by which members agreed to abide. As specified in these documents, tribes set up their own judicial

Secretary of the Interior Harold Ickes hands the first constitution issued under the Indian Reorganization Act to delegates of the Confederated Tribes of the Flathead Indian Reservation.

Bitter Anniversary

In 1967, Salish chief Dan George gave a speech in Vancouver, British Columbia, commemorating the one-hundredth anniversary of the founding of Canada. The following passage, quoted in *Touch the Earth*, written by T. C. McCluhan, does not speak so much of celebration as it does of the grief of the native people removed from their homes and forced to change ancestral traditions.

"How long have I known you, oh Canada? A hundred years? Yes, a hundred years. . . . And today, when you celebrate your hundred years, oh Canada, I am sad for all the Indian people throughout the land.

For I have known you when your forests were mine; when they gave me my meat and my clothing. I have known you in your streams and rivers where your fish flashed and danced in the sun, where the waters said come, come and eat of my abundance. I have known you in the freedom of your winds. And my spirit like the winds, once roamed your good lands.

But in the long hundred years since the white man came, I have seen my freedom disappear like the salmon going mysteriously out to sea. The white man's strange customs which I could not understand, pressed down upon me until I could no longer breathe.

When I fought to protect my land and my home, I was called a savage. When I neither understood nor welcomed this way of life, I was called lazy. When I tried to rule my people, I was stripped of my authority. . . .

Oh, God in Heaven! Give me back the courage of the olden Chiefs. Let me wrestle with my surroundings. . . . Let me humbly accept this new culture and through it rise up and go on."

---

systems and organized committees to govern such areas as education and health care.

Serving as a member of a tribal council was a challenging job. Council members not only had to work within the constitution and bylaws of their own tribes, but also had to familiarize themselves with numerous overlapping federal laws governing the tribe. These divided loyalties often put them in difficult positions and caused unavoidable delays in decision making and in carrying out tribal business.

Over time, the federal government held less jurisdiction over Plateau Indian matters. The Bureau of Indian Affairs loosened its control over programs and policies, but continued to help the Indians facilitate long-needed educational, economic, and social improvements on the reservations.

By the middle of the twentieth century, significant philosophical changes had taken place in the U.S. government's attitude toward Native Americans. In 1946, the government established the Indian Claims Commission to process claims that Indian tribes had filed against them. Most of the money promised to the Plateau tribes in treaties had never been awarded. The Nez Percé studied maps of their former territory and determined that the government owed them $20 million for lost land and gold mined from the land. In 1959, the Claims Commission awarded them the money. In 1965, the Confederated Tribes of the Kootenai and Salish won an award of $5.3 million for land turned over to the government in 1859. In 1951, after years of legal battles, the Indian Claims Commission awarded the Spokane $6.7 million for land they ceded under an agreement in 1887.

Modern Relocation Programs

Many tribal members left the reservations because the means for subsistence were so limited. Government relocation programs appeared attractive in the 1950s and 1960s. The programs sent Indians to urban areas to acquire skills and training. Since few of the promised job opportunities were actually available, however, many families became stranded in cities, obliged to compete for jobs with other struggling city dwellers. The relocation programs also further depleted the reservation populations.

In the last several decades of the twentieth century, Plateau tribes have witnessed many changes. They have rallied to boost their local economies as well as to preserve the remnants of their tribal cultures.

Chapter 7

The Tribes Today

Today, small but strong remnant populations of most of the Plateau tribes still live on reservations in the region. Though their lives have changed significantly, the tribes strive to maintain the knowledge and understanding of their elders.

A Plateau Roll Call

The Nez Percé people live generally on two reservation sites. Descendants of Chief Joseph and the others sent to the Colville reservation in Washington State instead of their former homeland of Idaho still live there. Most of the Nez Percé—roughly 3,500—live on a reservation in the city of Lapwai, Idaho. This 88,314-acre reservation lies along U.S. Highway 12 east of Lewiston.

About 525 Coeur d'Alene Indians now live on 69,299 acres of land in Benewah and Kootenai Counties in Idaho. However, only about one-quarter of the reservation land is tribally owned. Like the Nez Percé, some of the Coeur d'Alene people now live on the Colville reservation as well.

The Yakima tribe now consists of about 8,000 members. Of these, about 5,000 people live on the 866,445-acre reservation. The reservation lies about four miles from the town of Yakima, Washington, along U.S. Highway 97. The Cascade Mountains and sacred Mount Adams rise just to the west. A good portion of the Yakima reservation is off-limits to outsiders. Its winding roads lead to ancient root- and berry-collecting grounds, hunting areas, and tribal rangeland.

About 2,150 Spokane people are currently enrolled as tribal members. They live on reservation land in and around Wellpinit, Washington, where tribal headquarters are located. The reservation consists of 154,000 acres in eastern Washington on the north bank of the Spokane River northwest of Spokane.

The Indians of the Confederated Tribes of the Umatilla Indian Reservation now live on 172,000 acres in northeastern Oregon. Made up of members of three tribes—the Cayuse, Umatilla, and Walla Walla—the

Umatilla tribe now has about 2,200 enrolled members. About two-thirds live on or near the reservation headquarters in Pendleton, Oregon.

Today, the Confederated Salish and Kootenai Tribes of the Flathead Indian Nation are made up of about 6,800 members. About 4,000 of these people live on a 1,250,000-acre reservation in western Montana along the southern end of Flathead Lake. The tribal members on the reservation are outnumbered by non-Indians by about 4 to 1.

The middle and upper bands of many British Columbia Interior Salish tribes now live on the Canadian equivalent of U.S. reservations, called reserves. Roughly 1,000 middle Kootenai people live on five reserves in southern British Columbia. Several bands of Lillooet, numbering about 2,500, also live on reserves in British Columbia. The Okanagan people now live on a cluster of six reserves in Canada and have a population of about 1,500. The Thompson Indian tribe is now made up of fifteen bands and about 2,800 people scattered throughout several reserves over a land area of about 100,000 acres in British Columbia.

Tribal Governments

Most of these tribes have a council form of government. Five to ten members are elected to the council, which then makes decisions for the tribe. Being an enrolled tribal member entitles a person to vote and hold office in the tribal government and to exercise the hunting, fishing, and other rights reserved in the treaties with the government.

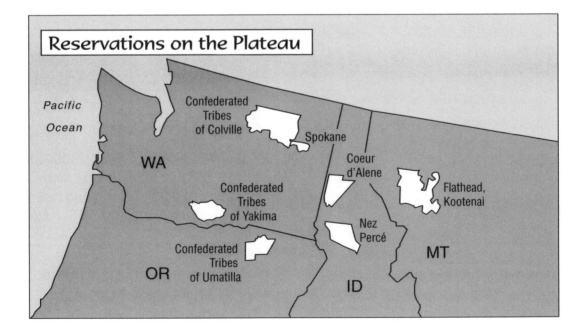

Reservations on the Plateau

In the middle of the twentieth century, most Plateau tribes adopted a constitution and bylaws, documents now used as a basis for decision making. For example, the Confederated Tribes of the Umatilla formally approved a constitution in 1949, which specifies that they are to be governed by a nonmember board of trustees elected by the general council. As with many tribes, the day-to-day operations of the tribal government are carried on by various departments, such as administration, tribal court, education, and finance, which are also staffed by tribal members. The Nez Percé created their tribal constitution in 1945, which specifies that the tribe is governed by nine elected officials called the Nez Percé Tribal Executive Committee. The Yakima constitution and government were established in 1933. The tribe elects fourteen representatives to a council that oversees eight committees, including timber, recreation and youth activities, and overall economic development.

Environmental Stewardship

Tribal governments take their role as environmental stewards of reservation land very seriously. Each tribe has its own department devoted to environmental protection. The Nez Percé call theirs the Environmental Restoration and Waste Management (ERWM) Department. They have recently undertaken a gray wolf recovery program for the U.S. Fish and Wildlife Service, managing a small population of the animals reintroduced to Idaho, since they were exterminated from the area sixty years ago.

Overall, the recovery program has been very successful. It has the highest breeding success rate of all three gray wolf reintroduction programs, including the most famous one in Yellowstone National Park. In fact, the program has been so successful that the wolf has been removed from Idaho's endangered species list. The Nez Percé feel that like them, the wolf had its home taken away. Because of this, they feel a kinship with the animals.

Hazardous Waste Cleanup

The ERWM has also taken on the responsibility of preparing for a large-scale environmental cleanup near the reservation. A nuclear weapons production facility in eastern Washington, called the Hanford Nuclear Site, which operated during the cold war, caused significant damage to the natural resources of the Columbia River region. A nuclear power plant also operated at the site for many years.

After two years of accumulating technical expertise in areas such as hydrogeology, wildlife biology, and hazardous waste reduction, the Nez Percé tribe is ready to begin nuclear waste cleanup contract work with the Department of Energy at the Hanford site. The Nez Percé believe that to fulfill their traditional role as stewards of the land, they must also undertake restoration and remediation of damage caused by others.

The Nez Percé tribal website explains their commitment to the project: "We are protecting our future generations by being

The Nez Percé and the U.S. Department of Energy are working together to clean up the hazardous waste produced by the Hanford Nuclear Site in eastern Washington.

integrally involved in the work itself, not merely the planning process. Building the technical expertise of our people will ensure that radioactive and hazardous materials will not outlive the Nez Perce people."[42] Should they be awarded the contract, the Nez Percé ERWM Department would ensure that throughout the cleanup, native archaeological sites and fish and plant habitats would be protected.

Other Environmental Battles

The Yakima people are in the midst of fighting environmental battles as well. Since the Enron Corporation declared its plans to build a wind generation plant on land they own on the Yakima reservation, the Yakima environmental department has sprung into action and prepared for a legal battle. If built, the energy generation plant would destroy one of the last places the

Plateau Artists and Entertainers

Many artists and entertainers are natives of the Plateau tribes. Among them are poet Debra Earling (Salish-Kootenai), novelist Janet Campbell Hale (Coeur d'Alene) and novelist Sherman Alexie (Spokane), winner of the American Book Award for his book *Reservation Blues* and author of *The Lone Ranger and Tonto Fist Fight in Heaven*, which was made into the movie *Smoke Signals*.

One of the most famous native American actors, Dan George, was a chief of a Salish band in Burrand Inlet, British Columbia. He was born in 1899 in North Van-couver, British Columbia, and died there in 1981. One of his first roles was the adoptive Indian father of Dustin Hoffman in Arthur Penn's *Little Big Man* (1970). For this role, he was nominated for an Academy Award. He also played the Old Sioux in the TV miniseries *Centennial* (1978). He starred as Clint Eastwood's fellow traveler in *The Outlaw Josey Wales* (1976). His other films include *Americathon* (1979), *Shadow of the Hawk* (1976), *Bears and I* (1974), *Harry and Tonto* (1974), *Alien Thunder* (1973), *Dan Candy's Law* (1973), and *Smith!* (1969).

Yakima people have for collecting important traditional medicines and foods. Also, the proposed site sits in the path of eagle and peregrine flyways. The large wind generation blades could kill the birds or interfere with their migration. Though the Yakima people acknowledge that wind-generated power is a good environmental alternative to coal- or gas-fired power plants, they think Enron needs to look at an alternative site that will cause less environmental impact. The Audubon Society and other environmental organizations have banded with the tribe, calling for another location to be selected.

Though they must fight legal battles with non-Indians who want to build large-scale developments on their beautiful reservation in northwestern Montana, the Flathead Indian Nation has won some environmental victories. A federal court recently upheld an Environmental Protection Agency (EPA) ruling that the Flathead Nation can be treated as a state and thus has the right to establish water quality standards within the exterior boundaries of the reservation. This means that they can regulate the activities of non-Indian people living on or near the reservation that could impact the water quality and fishing on the reservation.

Fishing Rights

Battles over water and fishing rights are some of the most crucial environmental challenges facing Plateau tribes. Though the federal courts have ruled that the Plateau people have a tribal right to fish at nonreservation sites, obstacles still persist. State police still arrest individual native people found fishing off the reservation and prosecute them in state courts. Plateau groups are also accused of lowering salmon reserves by non-Indian sportsmen.

To protect fishing rights granted them by the treaty of 1855, a joint group of Umatilla, Warm Springs, Yakima, Nez Percé, and several other Plateau tribes formed the Columbia River Inter-tribal Fishing Commission (CRIFC) in 1977.

The group not only defends its rights to fish in the Plateau region, but also works to restore dwindling fish populations in the area's rivers. In September 2000, the CRIFC published a vision paper, "Tribal Vision of the Columbia River Basin and How to Achieve It," detailing how they think the endangered salmon populations in the Columbia River Basin should be protected.

The vision paper raised governmental eyebrows because it called for adherence to and enforcement of all tribal, state, and federal laws regarding water quality and discharge permits. Specifically, it called for the halting of government subsidies

Several Plateau tribes are defending their rights to fish in areas off the reservations.

Salmon Restoration

Evidence of the Plateau people's success at salmon restoration is Salmon Corps. The program began as an AmeriCorps program with the goal of employing young Plateau Indian people to repair disappearing salmon habitats of the Columbia River Basin. "I've always been interested in fish and biology," said Daniel Jackson, an Umatilla volunteer, quoted in Emmett O'Connell's June 15, 1998, *Indian Country Today* article, "Salmon Corps Aids Indian Youth in Wildlife Conservation and Management Experience." "I've learned about fencing, barbs [fish structures] and the function of barbs. I've learned new skills." So far, Salmon Corps volunteers have built more than 395 miles of riparian or wooded fencing along the river, released over 7.5 million salmon, and assisted people living in flood zones.

One of the greatest aspects of Salmon Corps is that it invests in the environmental, cultural, and economic future of the Plateau tribes. It allows young people to get practical training for careers that will equip them to protect tribal land and treaty rights. Students also earn college credit at neighboring universities such as Portland State University for their work, and members who graduate get a five-thousand-dollar college scholarship.

given to corporate developments in sensitive areas like watersheds and floodplains that might impact the salmon populations. CRIFC executive director Donald Sampson says, "Put the fish back in the river . . . let them tell us what they need to survive. Let them sort themselves out, and they'll do that. But we've got arrogant scientists working for National Marine Fisheries Service that want control. And not only are they controlling fish, but they are controlling the tribe's efforts at restoring fish, which we've done successfully. And they are now controlling landowner's water use. They're controlling whatever they can. And it's not working."[43]

Sampson says that the CRIFC speaks from a solid base of practical knowledge and experience successfully restoring salmon to the Columbia River and its tributaries. "We have found we could restore salmon in many places where they are currently gone. We could rebuild the declining populations of salmon. We could improve the wildlife diversity and numbers in the basin and we could maintain the economy of the basin, if they managed the river differently and we used our resources more wisely."[44]

Tribal Economies

In the decades since having been moved to the reservations, Plateau peoples have rapidly developed and maintained tribal economies using skills that were once unfamiliar to them as hunters and gatherers.

For example, the principal industries of the Nez Percé are forestry, agriculture, and sand and gravel production.

Similarly, 90 percent of the Yakima economy is based on logging. The Yakima use carefully managed forestry practices to harvest trees on the one hundred thousand acres of the Cascade Mountains. They sell handmade wooden furniture at the Mount Adams Furniture Factory. In 1998, they opened Yakima Forest Products, the first tribally owned sawmill.

Some tribes are branching out from economies based solely on natural re-sources, however. After years of struggle and limited opportunity, the Umatilla are moving toward economic self-sufficiency by diversifying their economy. They now operate commercial developments such as a trailer court, grain elevator, and the Wildhorse Casino Resort, which includes a casino, hotel, RV park, golf course, and the Tamastslikt Cultural Institute.

The Nez Percé tribe also recently con-structed a commercial center, featuring a ten-thousand-square-foot conference cen-ter to house its gaming operation. They have also constructed a cultural museum

Bonnie Conner is the director of the Tamastslikt Cultural Institute, a facility that has strengthened the economy of the Umatilla tribe.

and an arts and crafts market to sell native-made goods to tourists.

Utility Companies

In an effort to make money and provide cheaper power to tribal members, several Plateau tribes have gotten into the utility business. In a joint project with the Eugene, Oregon, Water and Electric Board, the Umatilla tribe will build a $300 million power-generating plant. The Yakima also started their own power utility company in 2000. It will boost tribal employment, offering a training program for Yakima members who want to work as administrators, electricians, or salespeople. Though the Flathead Indian Nation leases the Kerr hydroelectric dam on their reservation from Western Montana Power, they will own and operate it in 2015.

Despite all these reports of economic progress, Plateau tribes still have a difficult time maintaining stable economies and holding down unemployment. According to Antone Minthorn, a Cayuse man who won the Northwest Indian Progress in Business Tribal Award, "Contrary to what some might believe, economic parity for the Native American community has not been reached. Only a small percentage of tribes are approaching economic independence. Most tribal communities still have 30 percent to 40 percent unemployment rates and unacceptable high school and college drop-out rates. . . . Building sustainable economies for our tribal communities requires a long-term approach,"[45]

Language Retention, Restoration

In the midst of looking to the future to ensure healthy tribal economies, Plateau people have also had to turn their efforts toward saving the past as well. This is especially true in the area of native languages. With fewer and increasingly elderly native speakers, each tribe is in danger of losing its native tongue. The language of the Kootenai, for example, is nearly extinct, with only a handful of native speakers. Though children pick up language easily, there are few adults fluent enough to speak it with them.

To address the problem, the Confederated Salish and Kootenai Tribes of the Flathead Indian Nation founded the Learning Lodge Institute, a collaborative effort between all seven of Montana's tribal colleges to save native languages. "The goal is to 'use education for the teaching of language and culture,'"[46] said project director Lanny Real Bird. Individual projects undertaken by the institute include certifying language teachers, documenting medicinal and ceremonial plants, developing language handbooks, sponsoring culturally based immersion programs, and creating partnerships with Head Start classrooms and public schools to instruct young people in their native language. "All this helps tribal communities reach a larger goal," said Real Bird. "It is part of each college's mission to 'empower the cultures so they can empower themselves.'"[47] This means that they can go on to become tribal leaders, managing their own educational, economic, and cultural programs.

Sweat Lodge is Sacred

When a non-Indian, Bud Cheff, wanted permission to build a sweat lodge in his museum at a resort in Ninepipes, Montana, the Salish opposed it. Writer B. L. Azure interviewed tribal elders for an article entitled "Salish Elders Oppose Museum Sweatlodge Exhibit Request" in the May 22, 1998, edition of the *Char-Koosta News*. "This is one of the few things we have left. It's hard to explain why you have to keep it personal," Salish tribal member Tony Incashola said. "The sweatlodge medicine and spiritual connection is lost when it is shared in such a public display. . . . If you believe in the religion (you know) by changing it, you destroy it. When that part of the culture is lost then your identity goes with it."

The institute's programs filter through to Salish and Kootenai elementary and secondary schools, which use a variety of means to teach languages to future tribal members. For example, language proficiency is required for graduation. Kootenai and Salish dictionaries are in the classroom. Mentor programs allow for students to speak their native language with elders. The schools also sponsor language immersion camps, where students speak nothing but their native tongue.

Indeed, many Plateau tribes couple language studies with a study of traditional cultural practices. For example, at Salish-Kootenai College, students work directly with tribal elder Johnny Arlee, who speaks fluent Salish. They live in the same camp with him; learn traditional ways of hunting, preparing, and sorting game; and gather roots and other wild foods. They also learn the traditional songs and ceremonies associated with these activities.

Similarly, at the Yakima Cultural Heritage Center, built in 1980, children and adults alike have the opportunity to experience immersion in the culture of their tribe's past. They spend time in a modern version of a winter lodge, where they can purchase locally made beaded buckskin clothes, pottery, and baskets. They can also learn basketry skills from older women and can go on trips to gather berries and roots in the traditional way.

The Powwow

For the Plateau people, the powwow, an annual seasonal celebration, represents a current expression of their spiritual life. In some ways, they carry on the ancient first fruit ceremonies and seasonal gatherings celebrated by their ancestors. In May, the

Nez Percé people at Lapwai hold a root festival powwow, where they play games and race horses with members of other tribes, just as their ancestors did. Similarly, each Labor Day, the Spokane host a celebration. They are joined by hundreds of people from other neighboring tribes for Indian dancing, stick games, and selling or trading handmade items.

Of course, over the years, the powwow has changed a great deal. Young people in-

A Salish tribe member dances in a powwow ceremony.

corporate many new and outside influences into their dances and costumes. Elders, such as Dolly Linsebigler of the Confederated Salish and Kootenai Tribes, believe that the powwow has suffered from "too many suyapi [white] ways that have been thrown in."[48] However, the young people take a great deal of pride in their dancing and in the powwow ceremonies. A young man from the Flathead reservation indicates just how important both the powwow and his elders are to him: "You are able to express your Indianness while you are out there dancing or powwowing or playing hand game. But young people do not learn Indianness from powwows, they learn it from their parents and elders."[49]

Historical Legacy

As the powwow illustrates, the past and tradition are extremely important to Indian people. Equally important to them is that an accurate and balanced history of their lives be presented for all to see. In preparation for the bicentennial of the Lewis and Clark expedition in 2003, a group of Nez Percé have organized the National Historic Trail Foundation, whose job it will be to present a different side of the story. "For native people, the Lewis and Clark exploration meant the opening up of the West and a dramatic change to their way of life," said Carla High Eagle, who is president of the group. High Eagle wants people to know that though her group will participate in the event, it is not a time to celebrate for them, "but a time to com-

In 2003, Carla High Eagle (standing) and the National Historic Trail Foundation will present the story of Lewis and Clark's expedition and explain how it affected the Plateau tribes.

memorate. . . . Telling the story truthfully . . . shatters a stereotype. . . . We are no mythical Hollywood Indian; we are real people who lived on the ground the Creator gave us."[50]

Umatilla at the Tamastslikt Cultural Institute, the first visitor center on the historic Oregon Trail, also want Americans to learn history from their, as well as from the settlers', point of view. "It's important in America that we have to realize the consequence of this migration we live with today," said Bobbie Conner, director of the center. "The rapid-fire change in our lives between 1840 and 1990 was overwhelming."[51]

The Plateau people have survived despite westward expansion and the disruption of a way of life they had lived for centuries. If their current progress is any indication, the tribes will continue to learn, strengthen, and grow.

Notes

Introduction: Hunters and Gatherers of the Northwest

1. Quoted in Jerry Todd and Jeremy Crow, "Nez Percé Tribe Goverment Structure," December 4, 2000, p. 2. www.em.doe.gov/stake/nez.html.

2. "Sacred Journey of the Nez Percé Transcript," September 21, 2000, p. 19. http://idahoptv.org/productions/archives/sacred/trans.html.

Chapter 1: Pursuing Seasonal Bounty

3. "The Flathead Tribe," www.omaha.lib.ne.us/transmiss/congress/flathead.html.

4. Colin F. Taylor and William C. Sturtevant, eds., *The Native Americans: The Indigenous People of North America.* New York: Smithmark, 1991, p. 101.

5. Quoted in Edward J. Kowrach and Thomas E. Connolly, eds., *Saga of the Coeur D'Alene Indians: An Account of Chief Joseph Seltice.* Fairfield, WA: Ye Galleon Press, 1990, p. 84.

6. Brian Hayden, *The Pithouses of Keatley Creek.* Fort Worth, TX: Harcourt Brace, 1997, p. 46.

7. Gail Hamlin, ed., *Dictionary of the Indian Tribes of the Americas.* Newport Beach, CA: American Indian Publishers, 1993, p. 40.

8. Quoted in Taylor and Sturtevant, *The Native Americans*, p. 102.

Chapter 2: Tribal Interactions

9. Confederated Tribes of the Umatilla Indian Reservation, December 4, 2000, p. 11. www.umatilla.nsn.us.

10. Confederated Tribes of the Umatilla Indian Reservation, p. 11.

11. Quoted in "The Confederated Salish and Kootenai Tribes of the Flathead Indian Reservation," December 4, 2000, p. 1. http://members.aol.com/Donh523/navapage/flathead.htm.

12. Quoted in "Lewis and Clark Meet the Yakima Indians" (selection quoted from *The Journals of Lewis and Clark.* Ed. Bernard DeVoto. Boston: 1953), p. 1. www.wellpint.wednet.edu/spokan/history/readings.php.

13. Quoted in David Wynecoop, "Children of the Sun: A History of the Spokane Indians," Wellpinit, WA: 1969, p. 6. www.wellpinit.wednet.edu/spokan/dance/dance.html.

14. Brian Hayden, ed., *A Complex Culture of the British Columbia Plateau.* Vancouver: University of British Columbia Press, 1992, p. 473.

15. Quoted in Taylor and Sturtevant, *The Native Americans*, p. 109.

16. Quoted in Taylor and Sturtevant, *The Native Americans*, p. 109.

Chapter 3: Plateau Spiritual Life

17. Julie Roy Jeffrey, *Converting the West:*

A Biography of Narcissa Whitman. Norman: University of Oklahoma Press, 1991, pp. 116–17.

18. Jeffrey, *Converting the West*, pp. 116–17.
19. Jeffrey, *Converting the West*, pp. 116–17.
20. Clifford E. Trafzer, *Death Stalks the Yakima.* East Lansing: Michigan State University Press, 1997, p. 40.
21. Quoted in William Kittridge and Annick Smith, eds., *The Last Best Place: A Montana Anthology.* Helena: Montana Historical Society Press, 1992, p. 91.
22. Peter Ronan, *Biographical Sketch of the Flathead Indian Nation.* Minneapolis, MN: Ross and Haines, 1890, p. 14.
23. Arlene Hirschfelder and Martha Kreipe de Montaño, *The Native American Almanac.* New York: Prentice-Hall, 1993, p. 111.
24. Kate McBeth, *The Nez Percés Since Lewis and Clark.* 1908; Reprint, Moscow: University of Idaho Press, 1993, p. xii.
25. Dayton Duncan and Ken Burns, *Lewis and Clark: The Journey of the Corps of Discovery: An Illustrated History.* New York: Alfred A. Knopf, 1999, p. 220.

Chapter 4: Early Interactions with Whites
26. Ronan, *Biographical Sketch*, p. 43.
27. Duncan and Burns, *Lewis and Clark*, p. 143.
28. Quoted in Wynecoop, "Children of the Sun," p. 8.
29. Quoted in Jeffrey, *Converting the West*, p. 43.

30. Quoted in Jeffrey, *Converting the West*, p. 89.
31. Quoted in Jeffrey, *Converting the West*, p. 148.
32. Robert Ruby and John Brown, *Dreamer Prophets of the Columbia Plateau: Smoholla and Skolskin.* Norman: University of Oklahoma Press, 1989, p. 10.
33. Jeffrey, *Converting the West*, p. 221.
34. Confederated Tribes of the Umatilla Indian Reservation, p. 7.
35. Jeffrey, *Converting the West*, p. 221.
36. Quoted in T. C. McCluhan, *Touch the Earth: A Self-Portrait of Indian Existence.* New York: Promontory Press, 1971, p. 56.

Chapter 6: Lost Lands, Lost Identity
37. Quoted in McCluhan, *Touch the Earth*, p. 10.
38. Wynecoop, "Children of the Sun," p. 13.
39. Quoted in Kittridge and Smith, *The Last Best Place*, pp. 357–58.
40. Quoted in Kittridge and Smith, *The Last Best Place*, p. 364.
41. Trafzer, *Death Stalks the Yakama*, p. 198.

Chapter 7: The Tribes Today
42. Todd and Crow, "Nez Percé Tribe Governmental Structure," p. 2.
43. Quoted in Cate Montana, "Tribes and Agencies Differ over Salmon Restoration Policies: Endangered Species Act Caused Sides to Adopt Divergent Views on Preservation," *Indian Country Today* (*Lakota Times*), September

27, 2000, p. C1.

44. Quoted in Montana, "Tribes and Agencies Differ," p. C1.

45. Quoted in *Indian Country Today* (*Lakota Times*), "Minthorn Recognized for Economic Development," December 14, 1998, p. B2.

46. Quoted in *Indian Country Today* (*Lakota Times*), "Save the Language, Save the Culture," October 11, 1999, p. C4.

47. Quoted in *Indian Country Today* (*Lakota Times*), "Save the Language, Save the Culture," p. C4.

48. Quoted in Johnny Arlee, *Over a Century of Moving to the Drum: Salish Indian Celebrations on the Flathead Indian Reservation*. Pablo, MT: Salish Kootenai College Press, 1998, p. 75.

49. Quoted in Arlee, *Over a Century*, p. 89.

50. Quoted in *Ojibwe News*, "Nez Percé Want Public to Know Other Side of Corps of Discovery," February 20, 1998, p. 2.

51. Quoted in Emmett O'Connell, "Ten Years After, Center Opens to Tell Story," *Indian Country Today* (*Lakota Times*), September 7, 1998, p. B8.

For Further Reading

C. J. Brafford and Laine Thom, *Dancing Colors: Paths of Native American Women*. San Francisco: Chronicle Books, 1992. This beautiful book provides stories and pictures of many Native American women, Plateau women included.

Ken Burns, *Lewis and Clark: The Journey of the Corps of Discovery*. Alexandria, VA: PBS Home Video, 1997. This beautiful video about the epic journey of Meriwether Lewis and William Clark covers their many encounters with the natives of the Columbia Plateau.

Vine DeLoria Jr., *Indians of the Pacific Northwest: From the Coming of the White Man to the Present Day*. Garden City, NY: Doubleday, 1977. Written by respected Native American historian Vine DeLoria Jr., this book provides a comprehensive look at the tribes of the Northwest, including the Plateau region.

Gail Hamlin, ed., *Dictionary of the Indian Tribes of the Americas*. Newport Beach, CA: American Indian Publishers, 1993. This excellent reference tool gives historical and cultural information on all native tribes in North and South America.

Idaho Public Television, "Script of Sacred Journey of the Nez Perce: A Co-Production of Idaho Public Television and Montana Public Television," September 21, 2000. http://idahoptv.org/productions/ archivbes/sacred/trans.html. On this website, you can read the script of a PBS documentary made about the Nez Percé's fight for freedom in the 1880s.

Andrea Lerner, ed., *Dancing on the Rim of the World: An Anthology of Contemporary Northwest Native American Writing*. Tucson: University of Arizona Press, 1990. Though somewhat dated, this anthology provides poetry and fiction written by many members of Plateau tribes.

Helen Schuster, *The Yakima*. New York: Chelsea House, 1990. This is a careful, scholarly, and easy-to-read account of the history of the Yakima people.

Victoria Sherrow, *The Nez Percé*. Brookfield, CT: Millbrook Press, 1994. A wonderful and accessible history of the Nez Percé and a look at the tribe today.

Clifford E. Trafzer, *The Nez Percé*. New York: Chelsea House, 1992. This book provides an especially thorough discussion of the final days and final battles of the Nez Percé before they were forced onto reservations.

Works Consulted

Books

Johnny Arlee, *Over a Century of Moving to the Drum: Salish Indian Celebrations on the Flathead Indian Reservation.* Pablo, MT: Salish Kootenai College Press, 1998. A wonderful book that gives a close-up look at the history of the Salish-Kootenai pow-wows.

Robert Bigart and Clarence Woodcock, eds., *In the Name of the Salish and Kootenai Nation: The 1855 Hell Gate Treaty and the Origin of the Flathead Indian Reservation.* Pablo, MT: Salish Kootenai College Press, 1996. Edited by modern descendants of the Salish and Kootenai tribes that fought so hard for justice during treaty negotiations, this book offers transcripts of the actual proceedings at the 1855 Hellgate Council.

Dayton Duncan and Ken Burns, *Lewis and Clark: The Journey of the Corps of Discovery: An Illustrated History.* New York: Alfred A. Knopf, 1999. A beautiful and scholarly companion guide to the PBS television documentary *Lewis and Clark.*

Gail Hamlin, ed., *Dictionary of the Indian Tribes of the Americas.* Newport Beach, CA: American Indian Publishers, 1993. A dictionary that describes the different Native American tribes in North America.

Brian Hayden, ed., *A Complex Culture of the British Columbia Plateau.* Vancouver: University of British Columbia Press, 1992. This book explores many aspects of the early history of the Plateau tribes of British Columbia.

———, *The Pithouses of Keatley Creek.* Fort Worth, TX: Harcourt Brace, 1997. Here, Hayden takes archaeological discoveries at the site of ancient Plateau villages and translates them into historical accounts of the life of a specific band of Salish people.

Arlene Hirschfelder and Martha Kreipe de Montaño, *The Native American Almanac*. New York: Prentice-Hall, 1993. This is a wonderful general reference for reading about any of the native people of North America.

Julie Roy Jeffrey, *Converting the West: A Biography of Narcissa Whitman*. Norman: University of Oklahoma Press, 1991. This book offers a detailed account of the life and ill-fated missionary work of Marcus and Narcissa Whitman.

William Kittridge and Annick Smith, eds., *The Last Best Place: A Montana Anthology*. Helena: Montana Historical Society Press, 1992. This anthology contains many stories told by Plateau elders.

Edward J. Kowrach and Thomas E. Connolly, eds., *Saga of the Coeur D'Alene Indians: An Account of Chief Joseph Seltice*. Fairfield, WA: Ye Galleon Press, 1990. Written by a Coeur d'Alene chief, this book offers the native perspective on many of the events and conflicts experienced by the tribe in the nineteenth and early twentieth centuries.

Kate McBeth, *The Nez Percés Since Lewis and Clark*. 1908. Reprint, Moscow: University of Idaho Press, 1993. This is an interesting account written by a Presbyterian missionary who worked with the Nez Percé and witnessed the end of the tribe's life off the reservation.

T. C. McCluhan, *Touch the Earth: A Self-Portrait of Indian Existence*. New York: Promontory Press, 1971. Though published more than thirty years ago, this book provides many beautiful photographs paired with words from Native Americans themselves.

Gregory Mengarini, *Recollections of the Flathead Mission: Containing Brief Observations Both Ancient and Contemporary Concerning This Particular Nation*. Ed. Gloria Ricci Lothrop. Glendale, CA: Arthur H. Clark, 1977. This is a scholarly text, narrowly focused on the experience of Jesuit missionaries to the Flatheads.

Peter Ronan, *Biographical Sketch of the Flathead Indian Nation*, Minneapolis, MN: Ross and Haines, 1890. Written by the Indian agent to the Flathead, this book provides an interesting look at the tribe and its customs from the perspective of an outsider.

Robert Ruby and John Brown, *Dreamer Prophets of the Columbia Plateau: Smoholla and Skolskin*. Norman: University of Oklahome Press 1989. Though a text for college-age readers, this offers an interesting examination of the rise of religious movements within the Plateau culture during the nineteenth century.

Colin F. Taylor and William C. Sturtevant, eds., *The Native Americans: The Indigenous People of North America*. New York: Smithmark, 1991. Provides a thorough discussion, complete with beautiful color photographs, of each of the tribes of North America.

Clifford E. Trafzer, *Death Stalks the Yakama*. East Lansing: Michigan State University Press, 1997. This book provides a thought-provoking look at the declining health of the Yakama tribe through the eyes of a historian and native Yakama.

Donald Worster, *River Running West*. New York: Oxford University Press, 2001. A biography of a naturalist and explorer of the Colorado River, John Wesley Powell, this book provides a rich context for westward exploration and the movement of the Plateau people onto reservations.

Periodicals

Sierre Adare, "Diane Mallickan: Nez Perce Park Ranger for the Nez Perce National Historical Park," *News from Indian Country*, December 15, 1999.

B. L. Azure, "Salish Elders Oppose Museum Sweatlodge Exhibit Request," *Char-Koosta News*, May 22, 1998.

Paul Boyer, "Learning Lodge Institute: Montana Colleges Empower Cultures to Save Languages," *Tribal College Journal of American Indian Higher Education*, January 31, 2000.

Char-Koosta News, "Ninth Circuit Court Rules in Favor of the Tribes and the EPA," March 6, 1998.

Lori Edmo-Suppah, "Native Beliefs Also Need to Be Taught in Schools," *Sho-Ban News*, September 30, 1999.

Troy Hunter, "Cultural Ecotourism–Ktunaxa Style," *Windspeaker*, June 20, 2000.

Indian Country Today (*Lakota Times*), "Minthorn Recognized for Economic Development," December 14, 1998.

———(*Lakota Times*), "Save the Language, Save the Culture," October 11, 1999.

———, "Yakima Upholds Their Sacred Lands," April 26, 2000.

David Melmer, "Salish-Kootenai Built Strength from Disparate Cultures," *Indian Country Today* (*Lakota Times*), October 11, 1999.

Cate Montana, "Hanford Reach may be declared national monument: Free-flowing stretch prime salmon water," *Indian Country Today* (Lakota Times), May 31, 2000.

———, "Nez Perce and Grey Wolf: Both Banished, They Recover Together," *Indian Country Today* (*Lakota Times*), February 22, 1999.

———, "Tribes and Agencies Differ over Salmon Restoration Policies: Endangered Species Act Caused Sides to Adopt Divergent Views on Preservation," *Indian Country Today* (*Lakota Times*), September 27, 2000.

———, "Umatilla Pioneer Cultural Resource Protection Coursework: No Shortcuts, 'Don't Expect the World,'" *Indian Country Today* (*Lakota Times*), May 24, 2000.

Ojibwe News, "Nez Percé Want Public to Know Other Side of Corps of Discovery," February 20, 1998.

Emmett O'Connell, "Salmon Corps Aids Indian Youth in Wildlife Conservation and Management Experience," *Indian Country Today* (*Lakota Times*), June 15, 1998.

———, "Ten Years After, Center Opens to Tell Story," *Indian Country Today* (*Lakota Times*), September 7, 1998.

Internet Sources

"The Flathead Tribe," www.omaha.lib.ne.us/transmiss/congress/flat-head.html.

"Lewis and Clark Meet the Yakima Indians" (selection quoted from *The Journals of Lewis and Clark*. Ed. Bernard DeVoto. Boston: 1953), p. 1. www.wellpinit.wednet.edu/spokan/history/readings.php.

"Sacred Journey of the Nez Percé Transcript," September 21, 2000, p. 19. http://idahoptv.org/productions/archives/sacred/trans.html.

Jerry Todd and Jeremy Crow, "Nez Percé Tribe Goverment Structure," December 4, 2000, p. 2. www.em.doe.gov/stake/nez.html.

Websites

"The Confederated Salish and Kootenai Tribes of the Flathead Indian Reservation," http://members.aol.com/Donh523/navapage/flathead.htm. This site provides detailed historical and cultural information about the diverse group of tribes now grouped under this single name.

Confederated Tribes of the Umatilla Indian Reservation, www.umatilla.nsn.us. This website provides an interesting and detailed perspective on the tribe's history and current culture.

"History of the Spokane," www.spokanetribe.com/tribe/history01.htm. This site provides a detailed history of the tribe, written by tribal elder David Wynecoop.

David Wynecoop, "Children of the Sun: A History of the Spokane Indians," Wellpinit, WA: 1969. www.wellpinit.wednet.edu/spokan/dance/dance.html.

Index

Rabbit-Skin-Leggins, 46
rafts, 33
raids, 35–36
railroads, 75–77
Raven, 30
Real Bird, Lanny, 92
Red River, 46
Reservation Blues (Alexie), 88
reservations
    Chief Joseph and Lower Nez Percé refuse to go to, 66–67
    creation of, 62–63
    current populations on, 84–85
    Flathead Indians forced to sell land on, 75–77
    suffering by Indians after moving to, 77–80
reserves, 85
Ronan, Peter, 19, 43, 48
rose hips, 18
Ross, Alexander, 46, 52
Ruby, Robert, 55

Sacajawea, 48
Sacred Heart Mission, 53
Sahaptin language, 54
Sahaptin tribes, 13–15
Saint Mary's Mission, 53
"Salish Elders Oppose Museum Sweatlodge Exhibit
    Request" (Azure), 93
Salish House, 51
Salish Indians, 61, 83, 85, 94
Salish-Kootenai College, 93
Salishan tribes, 12–13
salmon, 15–18, 40, 69, 73–74, 89–90
Salmon Corps, 90
"Salmon Corps Aids Indian Youth in Wildlife
    Conservation and Management Experience"
    (O'Connell), 90
Salmon River, 15, 69
Sampson, Donald, 90
Seltice, Joseph, 18
serviceberries, 18
Seven Drum Religion. *See* Waashat
Shadow of the Hawk (film), 88
Sherman, Tecumseh, 70
Shingah, 28
Shoshoni Indians, 31, 35–36
Shuswap Indians, 12, 17, 26–27, 33, 45
skirmishes, 35–36
Smith! (film), 88
Smith, Annick, 65, 68, 70
Smoholla, 57–58
Snake River, 15, 52
Snyder Act (1924), 80
song counter, 45
Spalding, Henry, 53–54
Speaking Eagle. *See* Black Eagle
spears, 15, 18
Spokane, 75
Spokane Falls, 65

Spokane House, 46, 51–52
Spokane Indians
    celebrations at powwows, 94
    current population of, 84
    DeSmet describes homeland of, 14
    fight in Indian War of 1858, 64–65
    learn about Christianity, 46
    location of, 13
    portable longhouses of, 22
    raids by, 35
    refuse to go to the reservation, 70–71
    selection of chiefs by, 31
    travels in expeditions, 36
    tribal organization of, 29
Spokane River, 13, 52, 84
spoons, 18
Steptoe, E. J., 64–65
Stevens, Isaac, 59–64, 72
Stevensville, 70
stories, creation, 37–38
sunflower seeds, 18
sweat lodge, 43, 93

takh, 41
Tamastslikt Cultural Institute, 91, 95
tawtnuk, 43
Taylor, Colin, 31
Teit, James, 40
tepee, 20, 22–23, 35
tewat, 42
The Dalles, 24–25, 53
Thief Treaty, 67
Thompson, David, 35
Thompson Indians
    boats used by, 33
    current population of, 85
    fishing techniques by, 17
    location of, 12
    roles of men and women, 26–27
    spiritual beliefs of
        origin of the salmon, 40
        potlatches held by, 45
Thompson River, 64
Tiloukaikt, 57
Timothy of Alpowa, 67
tiwatimas, 41
tmay, 28
Too-hool-hool-zote, 10
Toohulhulsote, 70
tools, 18
Touch the Earth (McCluhan), 82
Touchet River, 15
trade fairs, 9, 24–26
Trafzer, Clifford, 42–43, 78
trappers, 49
travois, 35
treaties, 60–63, 66–67, 75–76
"Tribal Vision of the Columbia River Basin and How to

Picture Credits

About the Author

Kelly L. Barth is a freelance writer living in Lawrence, Kansas. Her other Lucent titles include *Birds of Prey* and *Snakes* in the Endangered Animals and Habitats series.